Primary 2B
Preface

Primary Mathematics Intensive Practice is a series of 12 books written to provide challenging supplementary material for Singapore's Primary Mathematics,

The primary objective of this series of books is to help students generate greater interest in mathematics and gain more confidence in solving mathematical problems. To achieve this, special features are incorporated in the series.

SPECIAL FEATURES

Topical Review
Enables students of mixed abilities to be exposed to a good variety of questions which are of varying levels of difficulty so as to help them develop a better understanding of mathematical concepts and their applications.

Mid-Year or End-Of-Year Review
Provides students with a good review that summarizes the topics learned in Primary Mathematics.

Take the Challenge!
Deepens students' mathematical concepts and helps develop their mathematical reasoning and higher-order thinking skills as they practice their problem-solving strategies.

More Challenging Problems
Stimulate students' interest through challenging and thought-provoking problems which encourage them to think critically and creatively as they apply their knowledge and experience in solving these problems.

Why this Series?
Students will find this series of books a good complement and supplement to the Primary Mathematics textbooks and workbooks. The comprehensive coverage certainly makes this series a valuable resource for teachers, parents and tutors.

It is hoped that the special features in this series of books will inspire and spur young people to achieve better mathematical competency and greater mathematics problem-solving skills.

Published by
SingaporeMath.com Inc
404 Beavercreek Road #225
Oregon City, OR 97045
U.S.A.
E-mail: customerservice@singaporemath.com
www.singaporemath.com

First published 2004
Reprinted 2005
Reprinted 2007

ISBN 1-932906-03-7

Printed in Singapore

Our special thanks to Jenny Hoerst for her assistance in editing the U.S. edition of
Primary Mathematics Intensive Practice.

Primary 2B
Contents

Topic 1: Addition and Subtraction (Mental Calculation)

Mental Addition Strategies

(A) Add the tens, then add the ones.

Example: 123 + 46 = 169

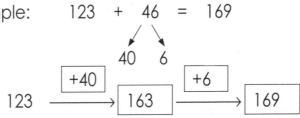

1. Use the above strategy to find the value of each of the following.

(a) 39 + 20 = _____

39 $\xrightarrow{\quad\boxed{}\quad}$ $\boxed{}$

(b) 45 + 34 = _____

45 $\xrightarrow{\quad\boxed{}\quad}$ $\boxed{}$ $\xrightarrow{\quad\boxed{}\quad}$ $\boxed{}$

(c) 112 + 43 = _____

112 $\xrightarrow{\quad\boxed{}\quad}$ $\boxed{}$ $\xrightarrow{\quad\boxed{}\quad}$ $\boxed{}$

(d) 123 + 24 = _____

123 $\xrightarrow{\quad\boxed{}\quad}$ $\boxed{}$ $\xrightarrow{\quad\boxed{}\quad}$ $\boxed{}$

(e) 245 + 45 = _____

245 $\xrightarrow{\quad\boxed{}\quad}$ $\boxed{}$ $\xrightarrow{\quad\boxed{}\quad}$ $\boxed{}$

(f) 81 + 12 = _____   (g) 67 + 11 = _____

(h) 52 + 43 = _____   (i) 24 + 67 = _____

(j) 58 + 28 = _____   (k) 95 + 26 = _____

(l) 74 + 67 = _____   (m) 59 + 92 = _____

(n) 315 + 11 = _____   (o) 437 + 62 = _____

(p) 167 + 24 = _____   (q) 246 + 36 = _____

(r) 368 + 14 = _____   (s) 425 + 67 = _____

(t) 517 + 24 = _____

(B)   Make 100.

Example:

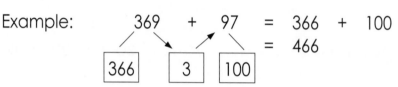

$$369 + 97 = 366 + 100$$
$$= 466$$

| 366 | 3 | 100 |

2. Use the above strategy to find the value of each of the following.

(a)   123 + 99 = 122 + 100 = _____

| 122 | 1 | 100 |

(b)   527 + 98 = _____ + 100 = _____

| | 2 | 100 |

(c)   246 + 97 = _____ + _____ = _____

| | | |

(d)   345 + 96 = _____ + _____ = _____

| | | |

(e)   418 + 95 = _____ + _____ = _____

| | | |

(f)   152 + 99 = _____ + _____ = _____

(g)   246 + 98 = _____ + _____ = _____

(h)   710 + 97 = _____ + _____ = _____

(i)   864 + 96 = _____ + _____ = _____

(j)   667 + 95 = _____ + _____ = _____

(k)   548 + 94 = _____ + _____ = _____

(l)   339 + 93 = _____ + _____ = _____

(m) 429 + 92 = _____ + _____ = _____

(n)   310 + 91 = _____ + _____ = _____

(o)   228 + 99 = _____ + _____ = _____

(p)   467 + 98 = _____ + _____ = _____

(q)   766 + 97 = _____ + _____ = _____

(r)   689 + 96 = _____ + _____ = _____

(s)   415 + 95 = _____ + _____ = _____

(t)   527 + 91 = _____ + _____ = _____

Mental Subtraction Strategies

(A)   Subtract the tens, then subtract the ones.

Example: $668 - 52 = 616$

3.   Use the above strategy to find the value of each of the following.

(a) $48 - 23 =$ _____

(b) 89 – 57 = _____

(c) 245 – 23 = _____

(d) 678 – 19 = _____

(e) 567 – 42 = _____

567 →☐ ☐ →☐ ☐

(f) 197 – 43 = _____   (g) 135 – 24 = _____

(h) 269 – 37 = _____   (i) 378 – 47 = _____

(j) 462 – 41 = _____   (k) 524 – 13 = _____

(l) 668 – 69 = _____   (m) 799 – 49 = _____

(n) 867 – 39 = _____   (o) 999 – 45 = _____

(p) 236 – 17 = _____   (q) 345 – 18 = _____

(r) 462 – 47 = _____   (s) 523 – 19 = _____

(t) 676 – 58 = _____

(B) Subtract from 100.

Example: 704   –   99   =   604   +   1
                                 =   605

604   100

Step 1:   100   –   99   =   1

Step 2:   604   +   1   =   <u>605</u>

4. Use the above strategy to find the value of each of the following.

(a)   333   –   99   =   233   +   1

233   100   =   _____

Step 1:   _100_   –   _99_   =   _____

Step 2:   _233_   +   _____   =   _____

(b) 425   –   98   =   _____   +   _____

        =   _____

Step 1:   _____   –   _____   =   _____

Step 2:   _____   +   _____   =   _____

(c) 365 – 97 = _____ + _____ = _____

Step 1: _____ – _____ = _____

Step 2: _____ + _____ = _____

(d) 523 – 96 = _____ + _____ = _____

Step 1: _____ – _____ = _____

Step 2: _____ + _____ = _____

(e) 616 – 95 = _____ + _____ = _____

Step 1: _____ – _____ = _____

Step 2: _____ + _____ = _____

(f) 246 – 99 = _____

(g) 919 – 98 = _____

(h) 624 – 97 = _____

(i) 555 – 96 = _____

(j) 717 – 95 = _____

(k) 428 – 94 = _____

(l) 314 – 93 = _____

(m) 169 – 92 = _____

(n) 347 – 91 = _____

(o) 426 – 99 = _____

(p) 518 – 98 = _____

(q) 265 – 97 = _____

(r) 111 – 96 = _____

(s) 328 – 95 = _____

(t) 467 – 98 = _____

5. Work out all the problems in order to reach home.

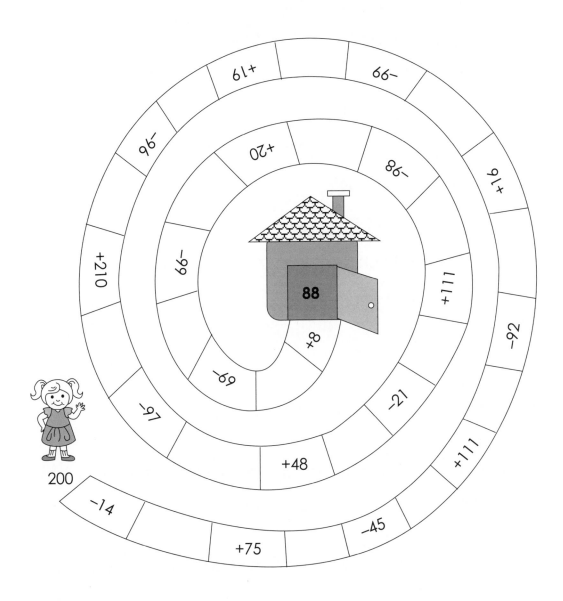

6. Fill in the blanks.

   (a) _____ is 23 less than 456.

   (b) _____ is 145 more than 225.

   (c) 615 is 99 less than _____.

   (d) 542 is 31 more than _____.

(e)　246 is _____ less than 485.

(f)　135 is _____ more than 19.

(g)　148 more than _____ is 600.

(h)　245 less than _____ is 112.

(i)　_____ more than 205 is 416.

(j)　_____ less than 512 is 501.

(k)　477 more than 99 is _____.

(l)　624 less than 998 is _____.

(m)　24 tens + 4 hundreds is _____.

(n)　42 tens − 2 hundreds is _____.

7.　Add 116 to 23. The answer is _____.

8.　Subtract 56 from 568. The answer is _____.

9.　Add 12 tens to 5 hundreds. Subtract the result from 90 tens. The answer is _____.

10.　Subtract 26 tens from 3 hundreds. Add the result to 9 hundreds. The answer is _____.

11.　Subtract 46 tens from 100 tens. Add 23 tens to the result. The answer is _____.

12.　Add 35 tens to 3 hundreds. Subtract the result from 10 hundreds. The answer is _____.

WORD PROBLEMS

Solve these problems. Show your work clearly.

1. After school, 87 children went for swimming practice. Eighteen of the children left the pool while the rest were still swimming. How many were still in the pool?

2. There were 23 boys and 48 girls at the zoo. There were 20 fewer children than adults.
   (a) How many children were there?
   (b) How many adults were there?

3. Mary made 240 cupcakes. She sold 99 on Monday and 98 on Tuesday.
   (a) How many cupcakes did she sell on the 2 days?
   (b) How many cupcakes did she have left?

4. John counted 126 apples on his tree on Sunday. On Monday, there were 99 apples on the tree. On Tuesday, more apples fell off and there were 23 fewer apples than there were on Monday.
   (a) How many apples fell off the tree on Monday?
   (b) How many apples were on the tree on Tuesday?

5. In a forest, there were 82 deer and 56 elk. Twenty-six deer ran out of the forest.
   (a) How many deer were left in the forest?
   (b) How many deer and elk were left in the forest?

6. May collected 125 polished stones. She gave some away and had 97 polished stones left. Later, her brother gave her 18 more.
   (a) How many polished stones did she give away?
   (b) How many polished stones did she have in the end?

Take the Challenge!

1. Draw a straight line (—, |, \, /) through 3 numbers that add up to the total given.

   (a) Total: 252

36	146	17
52	99	22
120	16	117

   (b) Total: 306

90	81	111
79	98	59
97	66	95

   (c) Total: 517

111	101	99
116	321	221
97	100	68

2. Fill in the correct numbers at the ends such that the total of any two end numbers gives the number in the middle of the line joining these two end numbers.
[Clue: Use 'guess and check' method.]

Example:

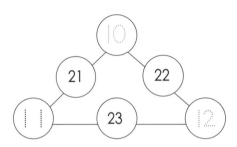

Check:
10 + 11= 21
11 + 12 = 23
12 + 10 = 22

(a)

(b)

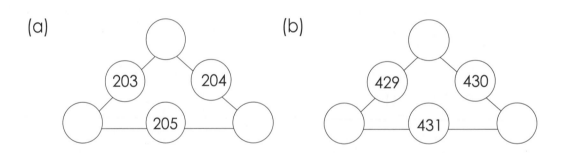

(c)

(d)

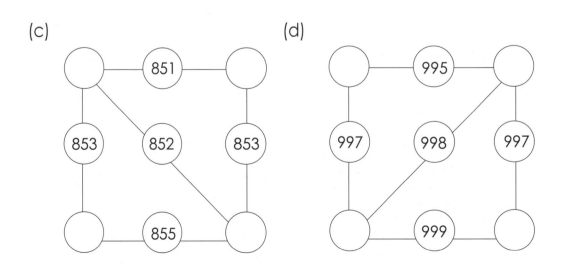

3. Fill in the correct numbers at the ends such that the difference of any two end numbers gives the number in the middle of the line joining these two end numbers.

[Note: The difference of two numbers means subtracting the smaller number from the larger number.]

[Clue: There are many possible ways. You may start by filling in any number at any one end.]

Example:

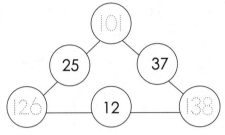

Check:
126 − 101 = 25
138 − 126 = 12
138 − 101 = 37

(a)

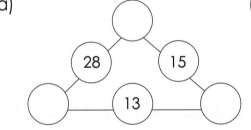

(b)

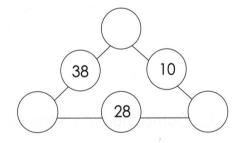

(c)

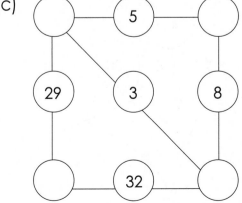

(d)

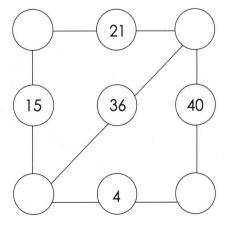

13

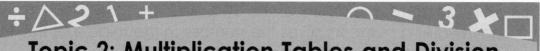

Topic 2: Multiplication Tables and Division of 4, 5 and 10

1. Complete the spider web to build up the multiplication table of 4.

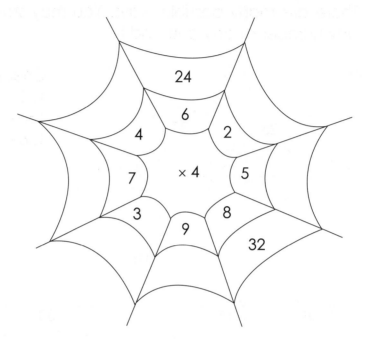

2. Complete the spider web to build up the multiplication table of 5.

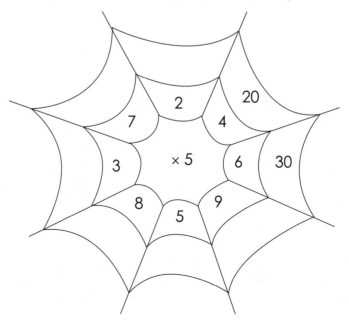

3. Complete the spider web to build up the multiplication table of 10.

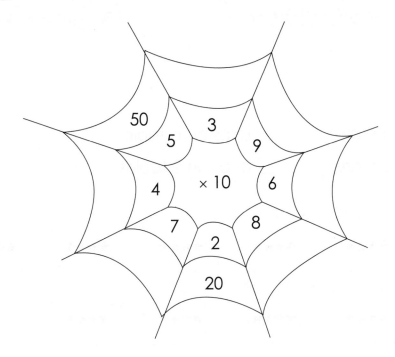

4. Fill in the blanks.

(a)

There are _____ flowers on a stamp.

There are _____ flowers on 3 stamps.

(b)

There are _____ coconuts on a tree.

There are _____ coconuts on 4 trees.

(c)

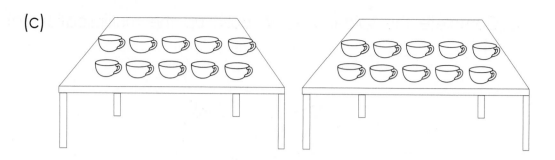

There are _____ cups on a table.

There are _____ cups on 2 tables.

(d)

There are _____ stars on a T-shirt.

There are _____ stars on 9 T-shirts.

(e)

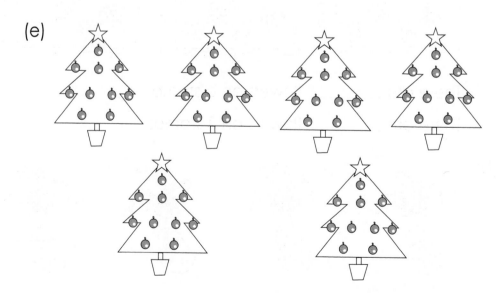

There are _____ ornaments on a Christmas tree.

There are _____ ornaments on 6 Christmas trees.

(f)

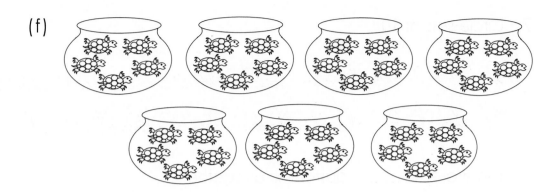

There are _____ terrapins in a bowl.

There are _____ terrapins in 7 bowls.

5. Circle sets of 4.

There are _____ flowers altogether.

There are _____ sets of 4 flowers each.

6. Circle sets of 5.

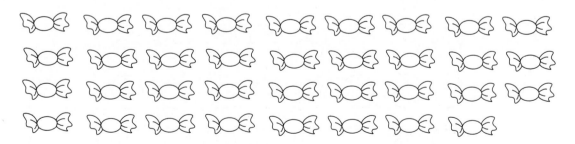

There are _____ pieces of candy altogether.

There are _____ sets of 5 pieces of candy each.

7. Circle sets of 10.

There are _____ butterflies altogether.

There are _____ sets of 10 butterflies each.

8. Circle 20 dresses into 2 equal groups.

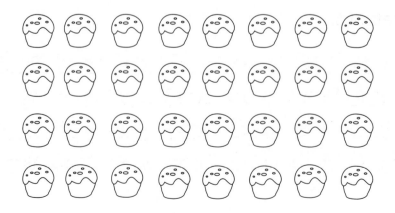

There are _____ dresses in each group.

9. Circle 32 muffins into 4 equal groups.

There are _____ muffins in each group.

18

10. Circle 20 caps into 4 equal groups.

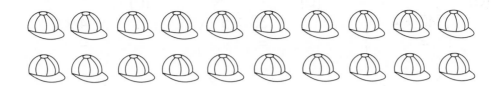

There are _____ caps in each group.

11. Circle 20 pots into 5 equal groups.

There are _____ pots in each group.

12. Circle 25 umbrellas into 5 equal groups.

There are _____ umbrellas in each group.

13. Solve the problems on the balloons.

(a)
40 ÷ 4
=

(b)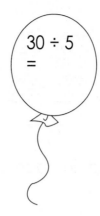
30 ÷ 5
=

(c)
4 × 2
=

(d)
5 × 9
=

(e)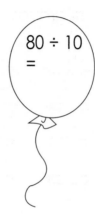
80 ÷ 10
=

(f)
4 × 9
=

(g)
36 ÷ 4
=

(h)
15 ÷ 5
=

(i)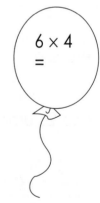
6 × 4
=

(j)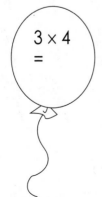
3 × 4
=

14. Complete the path by working out the answer to each step.

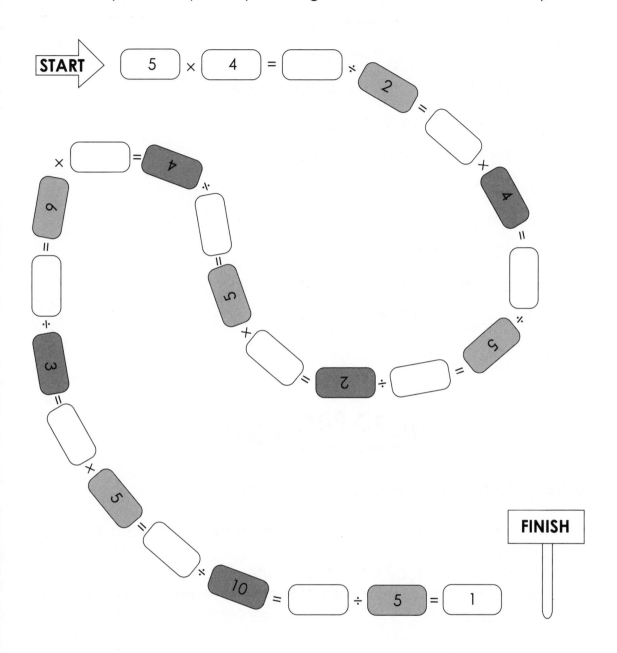

START ⟹ (5) × (4) = ( ) ÷ [2] = ( ) + [4] = ( ) ÷ [5] = ( ) ÷ ( ) = [2] + ( ) = [5] + ( ) ÷ [4] = ( ) × ( ) = [6] = ( ) ÷ [3] = ( ) + [5] = ( ) ÷ [10] = ( ) ÷ [5] = (1)

FINISH

15. Fill in the blanks.

(a) There are _____ fours in 16.

(b) There are _____ fives in 45.

(c) There are 7 _____ in 70.

(d) How many fours are there in 28? _____

21

(e) How many fives are there in 25? _____

(f) 7×5 is _____ more than 6×5.

(g) 8×4 is _____ less than 9×4.

(h) 10×5 is _____ more than 10×4.

(i) 2×4 is 4 more than _____ $\times 4$.

(j) 9×5 is 5 less than _____ $\times 5$.

(k) 4 more than 7×4 is _____.

(l) 5 less than 6×5 is _____.

(m) 10 more than 3×10 is _____.

(n) 5×7 has the same value as _____ $+ 10$.

(o) _____ $\times 4$ has the same value as $50 - 38$.

WORD PROBLEMS

Solve these problems. Show your work clearly.

1. There are 6 rows of tables in a classroom. There are 5 tables in each row.
   (a) How many tables are there in the classroom?
   (b) If there are 40 students in this class, how many tables are we short of?

2. Mrs. Pitt has 45 students in her class. She wants to have 5 teams of the same number of students for a swimming relay race.
    (a) How many students will there be in each team?
    (b) If 10 students are absent on the day of the race, how many students will there be in each of the 5 teams?

3. Marie made 228 mini fruit pies. She sold 196 of them and packed the rest into boxes of 4 each to give to her friends.
    (a) How many mini fruit pies did she keep for her friends?
    (b) How many boxes of mini fruit pies did she pack?

4. My doctor gave me 20 pills and told me to complete the medication. Five pills are to be taken each day.
    (a) How many days would I take to complete the medication?
    (b) If I skip one pill each day, how many days would I take to complete the medication?

5. May has 40 stickers. She has 4 times as many stickers as Carol.
   (a) How many stickers does Carol have?
   (b) How many stickers do they have altogether?

6. Ronny takes 5 days to finish reading a book. He borrowed four books from the library and would like to finish reading all four books.
   (a) How many days would he need to finish reading the 4 books?
   (b) If the library gives a 14-day loan to its members, can Ronny finish all four books by the due date? (Answer "Yes" or "No".) If not, how many more days does he need?

7. In a math quiz, 5 points were awarded for each correct answer and 4 points were subtracted for each wrong answer. Out of 10 questions, Amos had 8 correct answers.
   (a) What were the total points for his correct answers?
   (b) How many points were subtracted for his wrong answers?
   (c) What was his overall score for the math quiz?

8. In a box, there were 24 red marbles and 30 blue marbles. A total of 4 red marbles and 5 blue marbles were lost. Mark decided to put the remaining marbles in separate bags. He put 5 blue marbles and 4 red marbles in each bag.
   (a) How many marbles were left?
   (b) How many bags would he need?

Take the Challenge!

1. (a) If $\triangle + \triangle + \triangle + \triangle + 6 = 30$,

    what is the value of $\triangle$?

    (b) If $\square + \square + \square + \square + \square + \square + \square + \square + \square + \square - 8 = 62$,

    what is the value of $\square$?

2. At a farm where there are ducks and goats, I counted 52 legs.
    How many ducks and goats can there be?
    [There are many possible answers.]

Topic 3: Money

1. Match the money which have the same value.

(a)  111¢

(b) $9.90

(c) $2.20

(d)  140¢

(e)  425¢

(f) $0.99

(g)  201¢

(h) $8.12

(i) 615¢

(j) $6.70

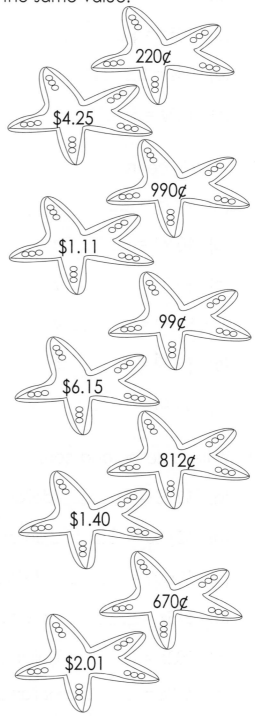

220¢

$4.25

990¢

$1.11

99¢

$6.15

812¢

$1.40

670¢

$2.01

2. Write in dollars.

   (a) 23¢ = $_____

   (b) 470¢ = $_____

   (c) 914¢ = $_____

   (d) 105¢ = $_____

   (e) 15¢ = $_____

   (f) 125¢ = $_____

3. Write in cents.

   (a) $0.75 = _____¢

   (b) $0.92 = _____¢

   (c) $0.05 = _____¢

   (d) $2.70 = _____¢

   (e) $5.72 = _____¢

   (f) $3.45 = _____¢

4. Write in dollars and cents.

   (a) $2.05 = _____ dollars _____ cents

   (b) $27.00 = _____ dollars _____ cents

   (c) $38.02 = _____ dollars _____ cents

   (d) 615¢ = _____ dollars _____ cents

   (e) 802¢ = _____ dollars _____ cents

   (f) 600¢ = _____ dollars _____ cents

5. Match the figures and the amounts of money in words.

(a)

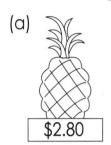

$2.80

Six dollars and
fifteen cents

(b)

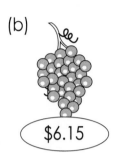

$6.15

Seven dollars

(c)

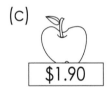

$1.90

Two dollars and
eighty cents

(d)

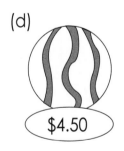

$4.50

Four dollars and
fifty cents

(e)

$7.00

One dollar and
ninety cents

6. Write each amount of money in numerals.

(a)

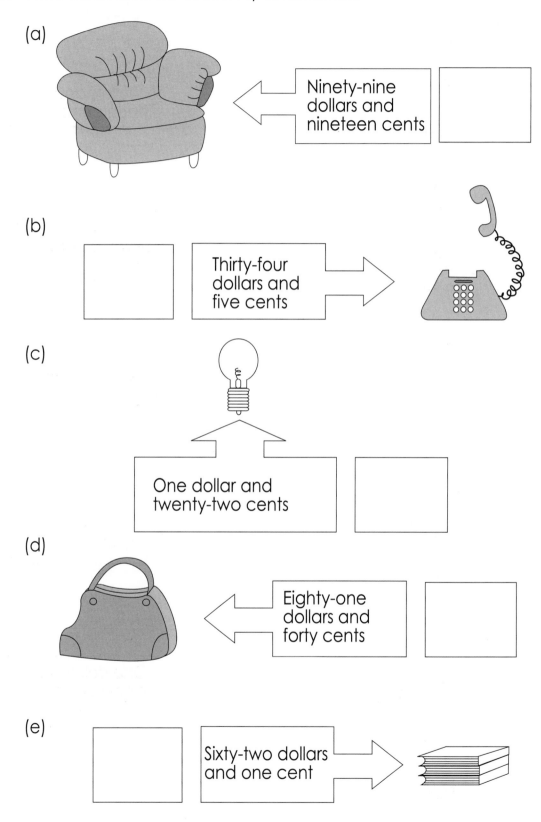

Ninety-nine dollars and nineteen cents

(b)

Thirty-four dollars and five cents

(c)

One dollar and twenty-two cents

(d)

Eighty-one dollars and forty cents

(e)

Sixty-two dollars and one cent

7. Count the money and write the amount in the box.

(a)
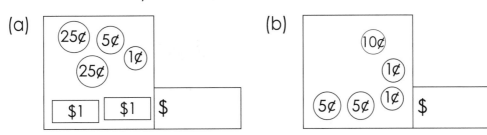

(b)

(c)
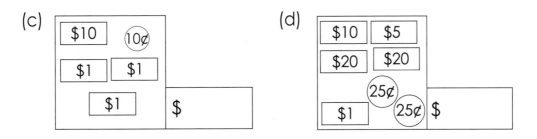

(d)

(e)
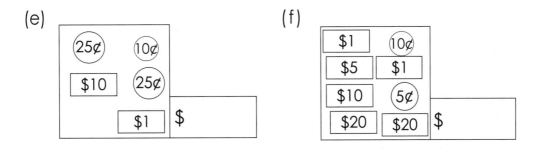

(f)

(g)
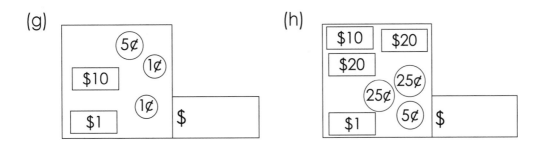

(h)

(i)
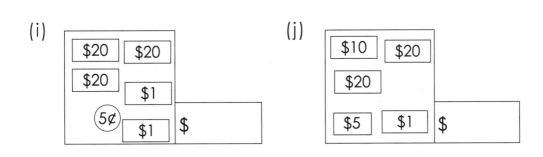

(j)

8. Color the bills and coins to make $26.35.

(a)
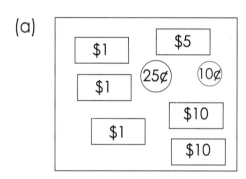

(b)
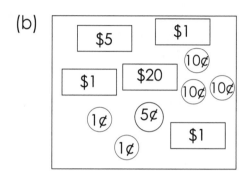

(c)
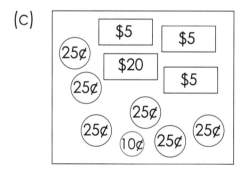

(d)
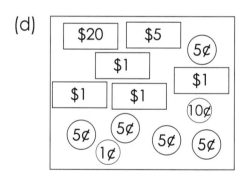

(e)
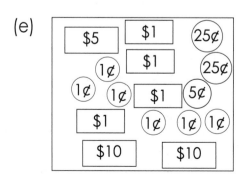

(f)
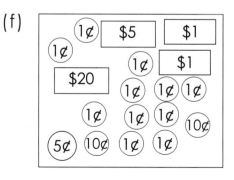

9. Fill in the blanks.

(a) $2.50 — + $3 → $_____ — +30¢ → $_____

(b) $1.40 — + $2 → $_____ — +50¢ → $_____

(c) $5.60 — + $3 → $_____ — +$0.30 → $_____

(d) $6.15 — + $0.30 → $_____ — +$3 → $_____

(e) $5.70 — + 25¢ → $_____ — +$2 → $_____

(f) $1.65 — + 15¢ → $_____ — +$4 → $_____

(g) $6.85 — + $0.45 → $_____ — +5¢ → $_____

(h) $4.01 — + $2 → $_____ — +99¢ → $_____

(i) $3.88 — + $0.02 → $_____ — +$3 → $_____

(j) $3.05 — + $0.98 → $_____ — +$3.00 → $_____

(k) $3.85 — −$1 → $_____ — −50¢ → $_____

(l) $8.60 — −$5 → $_____ — −65¢ → $_____

(m) $3.56 — −$2 → $_____ — −99¢ → $_____

(n) $9.99 — −99¢ → $_____ — −$0.07 → $_____

(o) $92.00 — −$22 → $_____

(p) $99.11 — −$9 → $_____

WORD PROBLEMS

Do these problems. Show your work clearly.

1. Rachel has $15.15. Her father gives her $20.
   (a) How much does Rachel have now?
   (b) If Rachel wants to buy a shirt which costs $36, how much more money does she need?

2. A home entertainment system costs $345. A wide-screen television set costs $310 more.
   (a) How much does the television set cost?
   (b) What is the total cost of the home entertainment system and the television set?

3. Judy went to the supermarket to buy food for her party.
   (a) What was her total grocery bill?
   (b) If she gave the cashier $40, how much change did she get?

Chicken wings	$23.50
Marshmellows	$4.00
Potato chips	$1.00
Candies	$0.50
Total	$?

4. Daisy saves $10 per week. Donald saves $6 less than Daisy each week.
   (a) How much will Donald's savings be in 8 weeks?
   (b) After 8 weeks, Daisy used her savings to buy a dress which cost $36. Who had more savings then and by how much?

5. Tom bought a pure-bred puppy for $250. At the pet shop, he spent $15 on a bed for his puppy, $1 on a can of puppy chow and $6 for a leash.
   (a) How much money did he spend?
   (b) The cashier keyed in the items wrongly and the bill showed $310. How much money did the cashier have to return to Tom?

6. Adrian had 5 nickels, 5 dimes, and some quarters in his piggy bank.
   (a) If he counted that he had $2 in his piggy bank, how many quarters did he have?
   (b) Adrian gave 2 nickels, 1 dime and 1 quarter to his sister. How much money did he have left?

7. Betty had 20 one-dollar bills, 4 five-dollar bills, 7 ten-dollar bills and 2 twenty-dollar bills.
   (a) How much money did Betty have?
   (b) Betty bought some story books and used up 4 one-dollar bills, 1 five-dollar bill and 3 ten-dollar bills. How much did she have left?

8. Mother gave Jack and Jill each some money. Jack bought a book for $4.95 and a pen for $3. Jill bought a ruler for 65¢ and a calculator for $7.30.
   (a) How much did Jack spend?
   (b) How much did Jill spend?
   (c) Jack had $2 left after spending on the two items. If Mother gave Jill $5 more than Jack, how much money did Jill have at the beginning?

Take the Challenge!

Circle the coins and bills below to get the value of $15.
All the money has to be used. You can find 10 sets of $15 altogether.

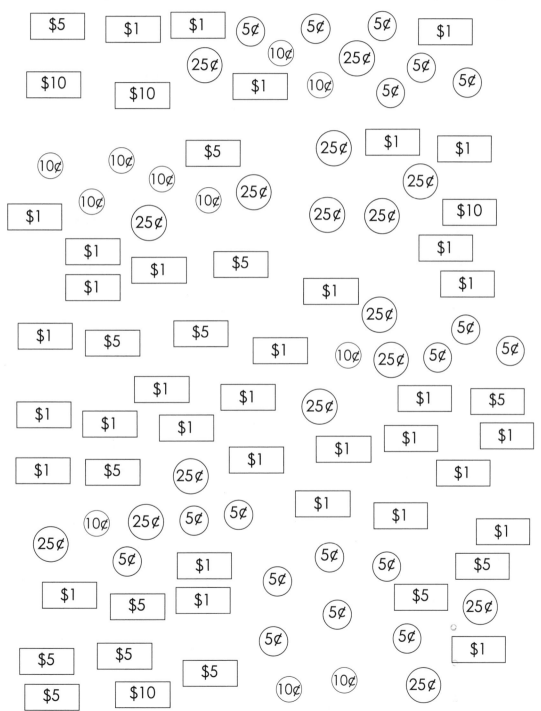

Topic 4: Fractions

1. Check (✓) the figures which are $\frac{1}{2}$ shaded.

(a)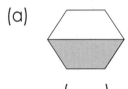

(   )

(b)

(   )

(c)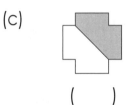

(   )

(d)

(   )

(e)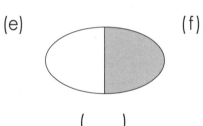

(   )

(f)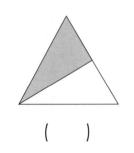

(   )

(g)

(   )

(h)

(   )

(i)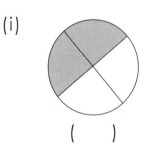

(   )

(j)

(   )

(k)

(   )

(l)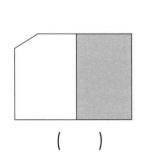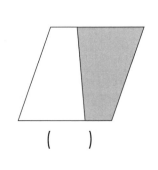

(   )

2. Check (✓) the figures which are $\frac{1}{4}$ shaded.

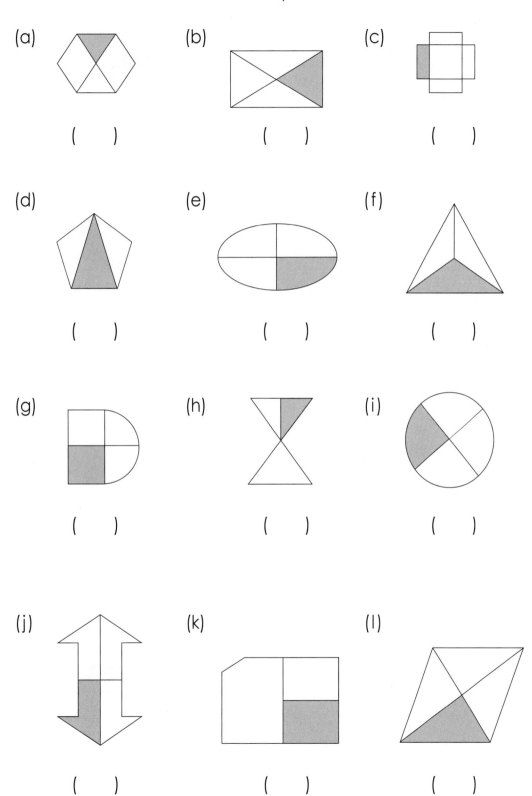

(a)

(   )

(b)

(   )

(c)

(   )

(d)

(   )

(e)

(   )

(f)

(   )

(g)

(   )

(h)

(   )

(i)

(   )

(j)

(   )

(k)

(   )

(l)

(   )

3. Name a fraction for each shaded part.

(a)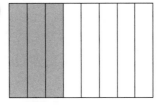

_____

(b)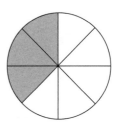

_____

(c)

_____

(d)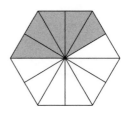

_____

(e)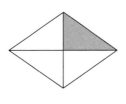

_____

(f)

_____

(g)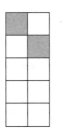

_____

(h)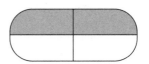

_____

(i)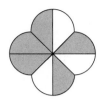

_____

(j)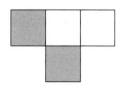

_____

(k)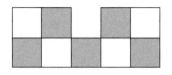

_____

(l)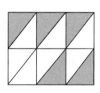

_____

(m)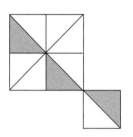

_____

(n)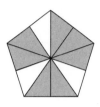

_____

(o)

_____

(p)

_____

(q)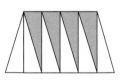

_____

(r)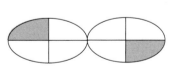

_____

(s)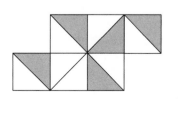

_____

(t)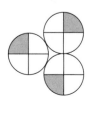

_____

4. Shade the figures to show the given fractions.

(a)

$\dfrac{1}{8}$

(b)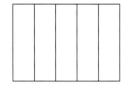

$\dfrac{2}{5}$

(c)

$\dfrac{3}{4}$

(d)

$\dfrac{1}{5}$

(e)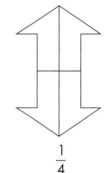

$\dfrac{1}{4}$

(f)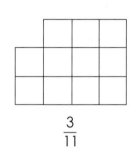

$\dfrac{3}{11}$

(g)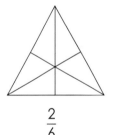

$\dfrac{2}{6}$

(h)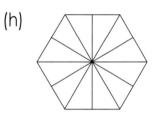

$\dfrac{3}{12}$

(i)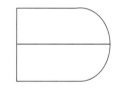

$\dfrac{2}{2}$

(j)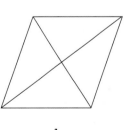

$\dfrac{1}{4}$

(k)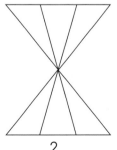

$\dfrac{2}{6}$

(l)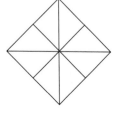

$\dfrac{3}{8}$

5. Color the animal with the smaller fraction.

(a)

$\dfrac{1}{2}$ $\dfrac{1}{3}$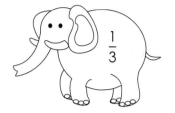

(b)

$\dfrac{1}{6}$ $\dfrac{1}{8}$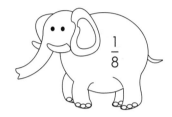

(c)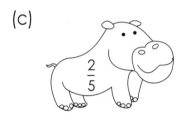

$\dfrac{2}{5}$ $\dfrac{2}{6}$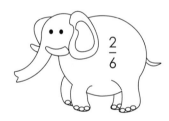

(d)

$\dfrac{5}{12}$ $\dfrac{7}{12}$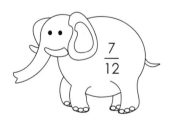

(e)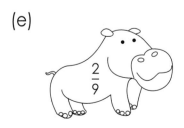

$\dfrac{2}{9}$ $\dfrac{3}{9}$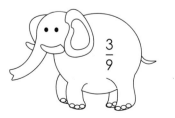

(f)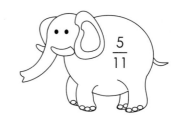

(g)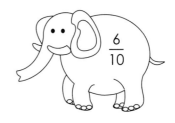

(h)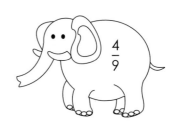

(i)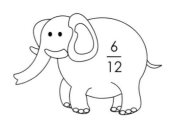

(j)

6. Color the animal with the bigger fraction.

(a)
$\frac{2}{3}$ $\frac{2}{5}$

(b)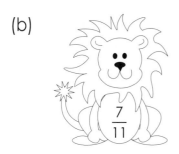
$\frac{7}{11}$ $\frac{5}{11}$

(c)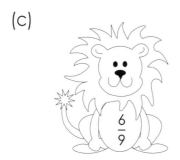
$\frac{6}{9}$ $\frac{5}{9}$

(d)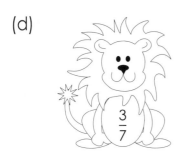
$\frac{3}{7}$ $\frac{3}{5}$

(e)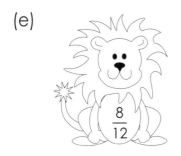
$\frac{8}{12}$ $\frac{4}{12}$

(f)

(g)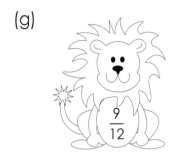

(h)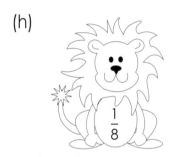

(i)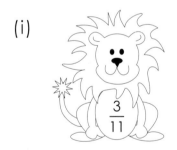

(j)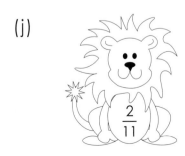

7. Join pairs of fractions that add up to one.

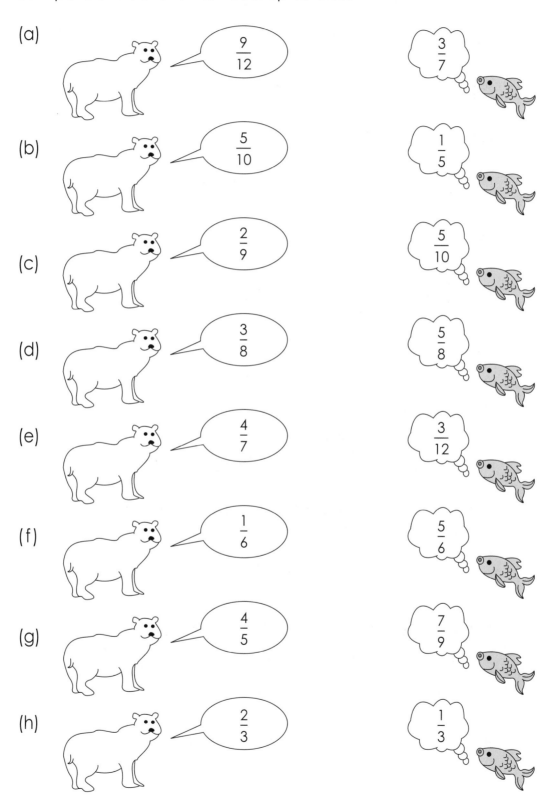

(a) $\dfrac{9}{12}$ $\dfrac{3}{7}$

(b) $\dfrac{5}{10}$ $\dfrac{1}{5}$

(c) $\dfrac{2}{9}$ $\dfrac{5}{10}$

(d) $\dfrac{3}{8}$ $\dfrac{5}{8}$

(e) $\dfrac{4}{7}$ $\dfrac{3}{12}$

(f) $\dfrac{1}{6}$ $\dfrac{5}{6}$

(g) $\dfrac{4}{5}$ $\dfrac{7}{9}$

(h) $\dfrac{2}{3}$ $\dfrac{1}{3}$

8. Fill in the blanks.

(a) $\frac{1}{8}$ = _____ out of _____ equal parts.

(b) _____ = 2 out of 11 equal parts.

(c) _____ is 5 out of 12 equal parts.

(d) $\frac{3}{8}$ and _____ make 1 whole.

(e) _____ and $\frac{4}{7}$ make 1 whole.

(f) $\frac{1}{4}$ and _____ make 1 whole.

(g) _____ and $\frac{1}{10}$ make 1 whole.

(h) A figure is divided into 11 equal parts.
3 equal parts are shaded.

We say _____ of the figure is shaded.

(i) A figure is divided into _____ equal parts.
6 equal parts are shaded.

We say $\frac{6}{10}$ of the figure is shaded.

(j) A figure is divided into 12 equal parts.
_____ equal parts are shaded.

We say $\frac{5}{12}$ of the figure is shaded.

(k) A figure is divided into 8 equal parts.
3 equal parts are not shaded.

We say _____ of the figure is shaded.

(l) A figure is divided into _____ equal parts.
7 equal parts are not shaded.
We say nothing is shaded on the figure.

(m) A figure is divided into 9 equal parts.

_____ equal parts are not shaded.

We say $\frac{2}{9}$ of the figure is shaded.

(n) 1 whole is made up of $\frac{2}{7}$ and _____ .

(o) 1 whole is made up of $\frac{5}{8}$ and _____ .

(p) 1 whole is made up of _____ and $\frac{5}{10}$.

(q) 1 whole is made up of _____ and $\frac{10}{12}$.

(r) 1 whole is made up of _____ and $\frac{7}{11}$.

9. Arrange the fractions in order, beginning with the smallest.

(a) $\frac{1}{9}$, $\frac{1}{10}$, $\frac{1}{6}$, $\frac{1}{11}$ _____

(b) $\frac{7}{9}$, $\frac{7}{7}$, $\frac{7}{8}$, $\frac{7}{11}$ _____

(c) $\dfrac{4}{11}$, $\dfrac{4}{6}$, $\dfrac{4}{8}$, $\dfrac{4}{12}$ _____

(d) $\dfrac{5}{9}$, $\dfrac{5}{11}$, $\dfrac{5}{8}$, $\dfrac{5}{12}$ _____

(e) $\dfrac{1}{12}$, $\dfrac{1}{11}$, $\dfrac{1}{6}$, $\dfrac{1}{7}$ _____

10. Arrange the fractions in order, beginning with the largest.

(a) $\dfrac{2}{3}$, $\dfrac{2}{5}$, $\dfrac{2}{7}$, $\dfrac{2}{11}$ _____

(b) $\dfrac{3}{6}$, $\dfrac{3}{4}$, $\dfrac{3}{7}$, $\dfrac{3}{8}$ _____

(c) $\dfrac{9}{11}$, $\dfrac{9}{10}$, $\dfrac{9}{12}$, $\dfrac{9}{9}$ _____

(d) $\dfrac{1}{4}$, $\dfrac{1}{3}$, $\dfrac{1}{5}$, $\dfrac{1}{7}$ _____

(e) $\dfrac{5}{11}$, $\dfrac{5}{9}$, $\dfrac{5}{12}$, $\dfrac{5}{8}$ _____

WORD PROBLEMS

Solve these problems. Show your work clearly.

1. Lisa cut a melon into 12 equal pieces. She ate 3 pieces and her parents took one each. What fraction of the melon was eaten?

2. Mother bought a blueberry pie and shared it equally among Father, Adam, Alexis and herself.
   (a) How many equal pieces did she cut the pie into?
   (b) What fraction of the pie did each person have?

3. Jane went to see the doctor who gave her a bottle of cough syrup. On the bottle are 12 equal markings. Jane was told to take a tablespoon of cough syrup three times a day. Each tablespoon is equal to one marking.
   (a) How many days would Jane take to finish the cough syrup?
   (b) What fraction of her cough syrup would she take in a day?

4. Ben and four of his friends bought a pizza for lunch and shared it equally among themselves.
   (a) How many equal pieces did they cut the puzza into?
   (b) What fraction of the pizza did his four friends have altogether?

Take the **Challenge!**

The shaded part(s) of each square is/are marked with value(s). Find the value of each whole square.

(a)
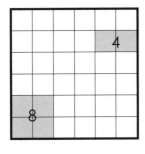

_____

(b)
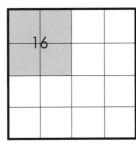

_____

(c)
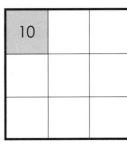

_____

(d)
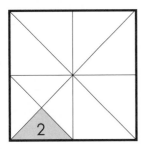

_____

(e)
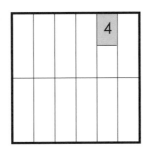

_____

(f)
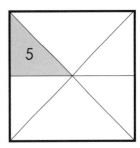

_____

(g)
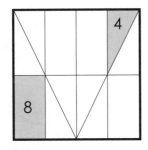

_____

(h)
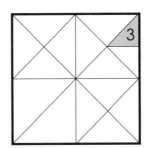

_____

(i)
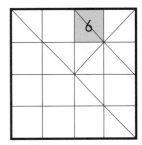

_____

(j)
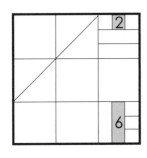

_____

(k)
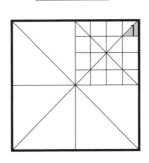

_____

(l)
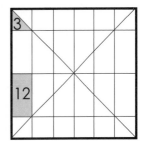

_____

1. Match the given time to the clock.

10:20	
12:50	
11:40	
12:15	
1:45	
4:10	

2. Write the time shown on the clock.

(a)

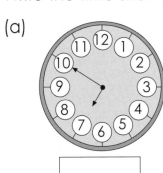

(b)

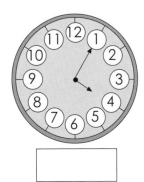

(c)

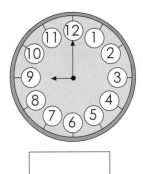

(d)

(e)

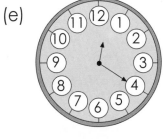

(f)

(g)

(h)

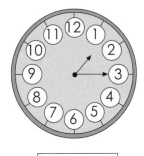

3. Write the time shown on the clock in words.

(a)

_____ o'clock

(b)

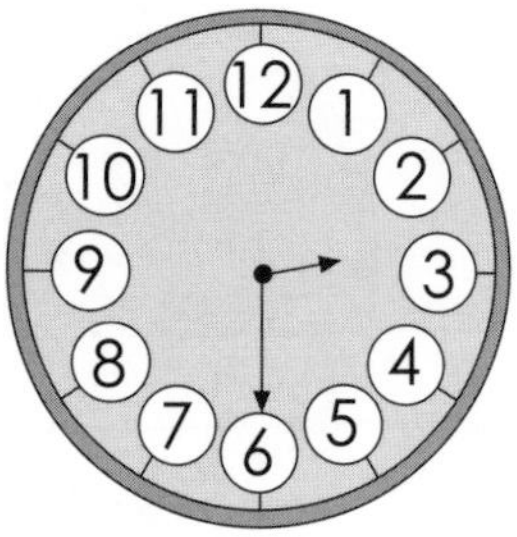

Half past _____

(c)

_____ minutes to five

(d)

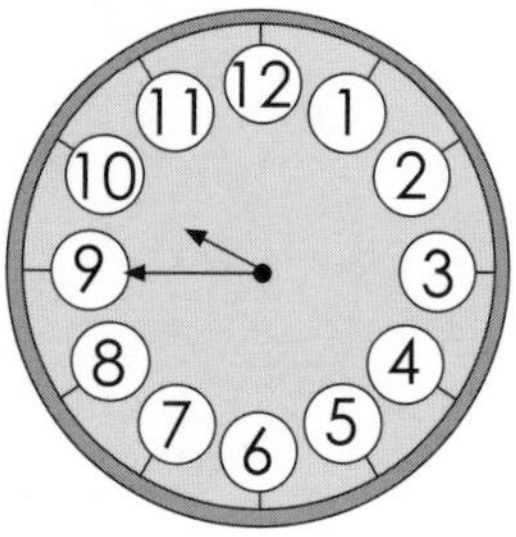

Fifteen minutes to _____

(e)

_____ minutes past ten

(f)

_____ minutes to one

(g)

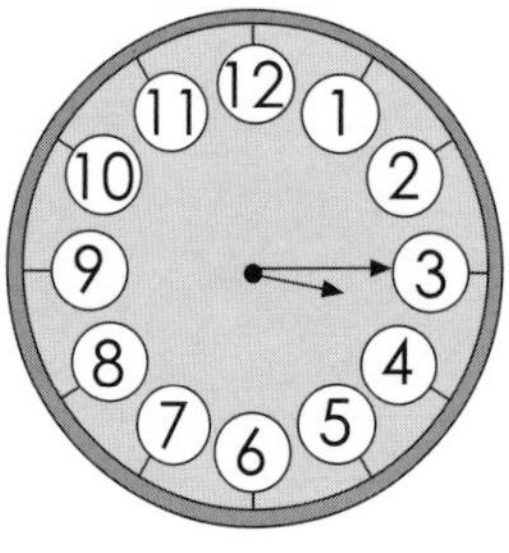

_____ minutes past three

(h)

Ten minutes to _____

4. Draw the minute hand on each clock face to show the given time.

(a) 9:50

(b) 2:20

(c) 1:45

(d) 11:10

(e) 5:35

(f) 6:40

57

5. Draw the hour hand on each clock face to show the given time.

(a)

| 4:05 |

(b)

| 10:10 |

(c)

| 11:15 |

(d)

| 7:50 |

(e)

| 8:30 |

(f)

| 9:55 |

6. Write the time using am or pm.

(a) 10 minutes to seven in the morning. _____

(b) Half past one in the afternoon. _____

(c) Quarter to six in the evening. _____

(d) Five minutes to two in the afternoon. _____

(e) 35 minutes past nine in the morning. _____

(f) Fifteen minutes to eleven in the morning. _____

(g) 20 minutes after five in the evening. _____

(h) Two minutes to twelve at night. _____

(i) 20 minutes before twelve noon. _____

(j) 20 minutes past midnight. _____

7. Fill in the blanks.

(a) 10:00 am   [1 hour later >]   _____

(b) 11:00 am   [< 1 hour before]   _____

(c) 1:00 pm   [1 hour later >]   _____

(d) 4:00 pm   [< 1 hour before]   _____

(e) 12:00 noon   [$\frac{1}{2}$ hour later >]   _____

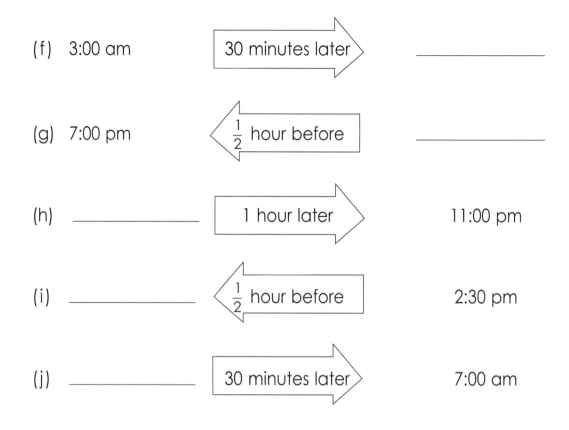

(f) 3:00 am 〉 30 minutes later 〉 _____

(g) 7:00 pm 〈 $\frac{1}{2}$ hour before _____

(h) _____ 〉 1 hour later 〉 11:00 pm

(i) _____ 〈 $\frac{1}{2}$ hour before 2:30 pm

(j) _____ 〉 30 minutes later 〉 7:00 am

WORD PROBLEMS

Do these word problems.

1. Mr. Singh finished playing golf at 10:45 am. If he played golf for 3 hours, at what time did he start playing golf?

2. Sharon was at the supermarket at 11:00 am. She spent half an hour shopping for groceries and was ready to make payment at the cashier. She stood in line for another half an hour and was ready to head for home.
   (a) At what time was she at the cashier when she completed her shopping?
   (b) At what time was she ready to head for home?

3. Adam and Eve reached the ticket counter of Rex Theater at 1:15 pm. They stood in line for half an hour to get their tickets. They then went into the theater just in time to watch a two-hour movie.
   (a) At what time did the movie start?
   (b) At what time did the movie end?

Take the Challenge!

All over the world, time zones are different in various places.
Use the time zones below to answer the following questions.

Time Zones

Singapore is 7 hours ahead of London.

Sydney is 3 hours ahead of Singapore.

New York is 5 hours behind London.

Los Angeles is 15 hours behind Singapore.

Singapore is 2 hours behind Tokyo.

Cairo is 10 hours ahead of Los Angeles.

Los Angeles is 4 hours behind Buenos Aires.

---

1. It is now 10 am in New York.

    The time in London is _____ .

2. It is 5 pm in Tokyo.

    The time in Singapore is _____ .

3. It is 12 midnight in London.

    The time in New York is _____ the day before.

4. It is 2:30 am in Los Angeles.

    The time in Cairo is _____ .

5. It is 4:15 pm in Buenos Aires.

    The time in Los Angeles is _____ .

6. It is 7:45 am in Singapore.

   The time in Los Angeles is _____ the day before.

7. It is 10:10 pm in Sydney.

   The time in London is _____.

8. It is 11:05 pm in Tokyo.

   The time in Los Angeles is _____.

9. It is 8:35 am in New York.

   The time in Singapore is _____.

10. It is 9:15 am in Buenos Aires.

    The time in Cairo is _____.

1. Fill in the blanks.

(a)

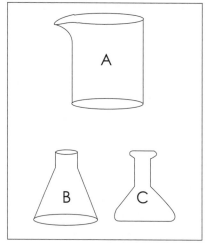

Container A can contain
more water than

Containers _____ and

_____.

(b)

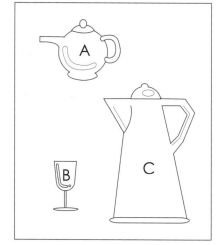

Container A can contain
more water than

Container _____.

(c)

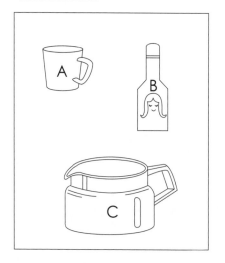

Containers _____ and
_____ can contain
less water than Container C.

(d)

Container _____ can
contain less water than
Container A.

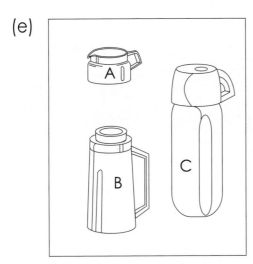

(e)

Container B can contain
less water than Container

_____.

2. Write the amount of water in each container in the boxes.

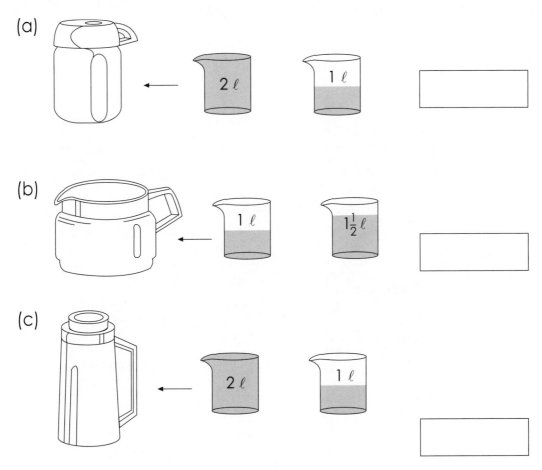

(a)

(b)

(c)

(d)

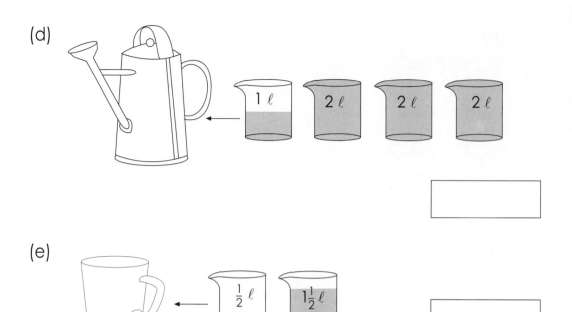

(e)

3. Write the amount of water in each container.

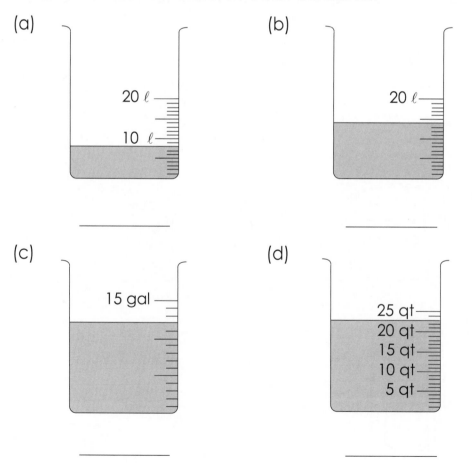

(a)

20 ℓ —
10 ℓ —

_____

(b)

20 ℓ —

_____

(c)

15 gal —

_____

(d)

25 qt —
20 qt —
15 qt —
10 qt —
5 qt —

_____

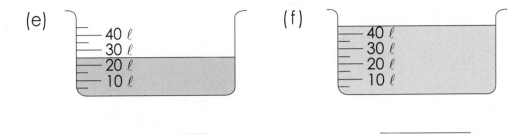

(e) _____

(f) _____

4. Fill in the blanks.

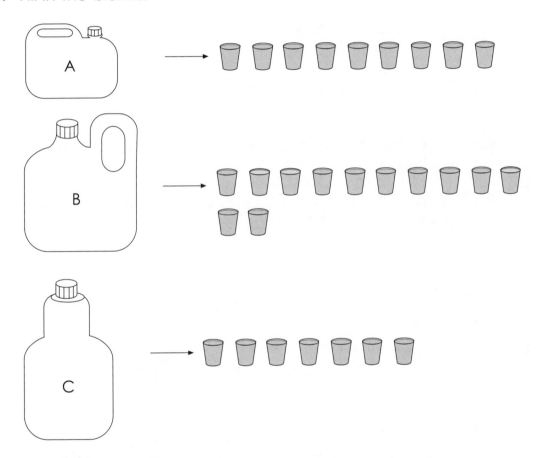

(a) Container A contains _____ glasses of water.

(b) Container B contains _____ glasses of water more than Container C.

(c) Container C contains _____ glasses of water less than Container A.

(d) Containers A, B and C contain _____ glasses of water altogether.

67

5.

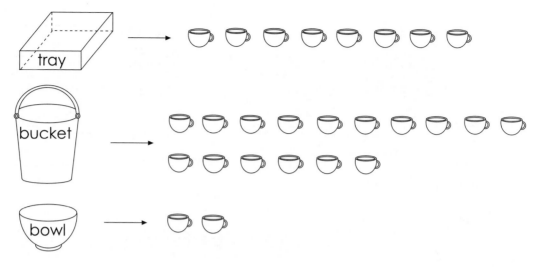

(a) The _____ can contain 6 cups of water more than the bowl.

(b) The bucket can contain _____ cups of water more than the tray.

(c) The bucket can contain _____ cups of water more than the tray and the bowl together.

6.

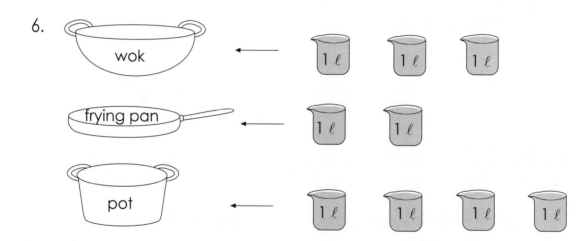

(a) The _____ is filled with one liter of water less than the wok.

(b) The _____ is filled with one liter of water more than the wok.

(c) Together, the frying pan and pot are filled with _____ liters of water.

7.

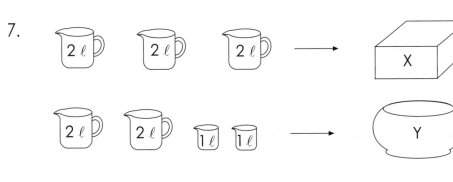

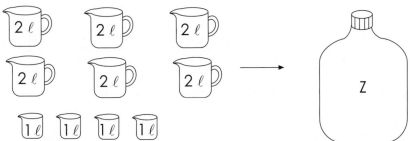

(a) Container _____ and Container _____ contain the same amount of water.

(b) Container Z contains _____ liter(s) of water.

(c) Two of Container X contain _____ liter(s) of water altogether.

(d) Three of Container Y contain _____ liter(s) of water altogether.

8.

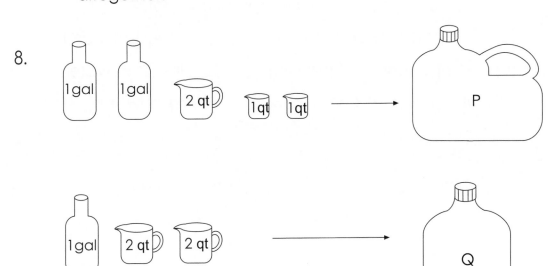

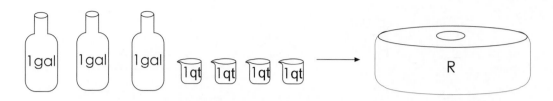

(a) The volume of water in Container P is _____ gallon(s).

(b) Container P contains _____ gallon(s) of water less than Container R.

(c) Containers P and Q contain _____ gallon(s) of water more than Container R.

(d) The total volume of water in all three containers is _____ gallon(s).

9.

(a) _____ glasses of water can fill one pot.

(b) Two pots can be filled with _____ liter(s) of water.

(c) One pot can be filled with _____ liter(s) of water.

(d) One glass can contain _____ liter(s) of water.

10.

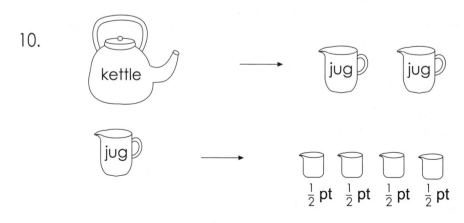

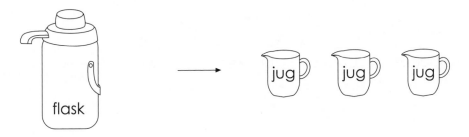

(a) A jug contains _____ pint(s) of water.

(b) A kettle contains _____ pints(s) of water.

(c) A flask contains _____ pints(s) of water more than a jug.

(d) Four jugs and a flask together contain _____ pints(s) of water.

11.

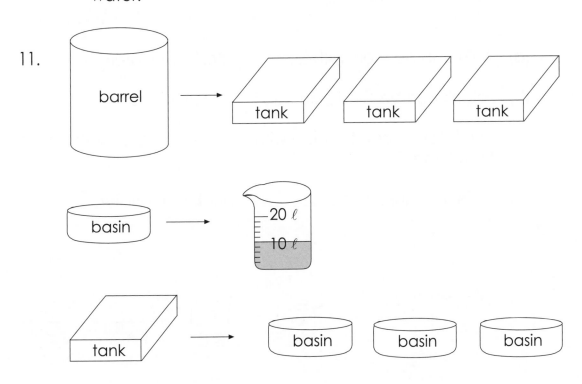

(a) A basin contains _____ liter(s) of water.

(b) A barrel contains _____ liter(s) of water.

(c) To fill two tanks, I need _____ liter(s) of water.

(d) To fill six basins of water, I need _____ tanks of water.

12.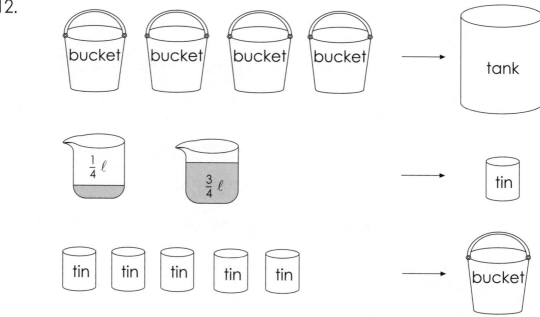

(a) A tin can be filled with _____ liter(s) of water.

(b) A tank can be filled with _____ liters of water.

(c) Two buckets can be filled with _____ liters of water more than three tins.

(d) To fill ten tanks, I need _____ buckets of water.

13.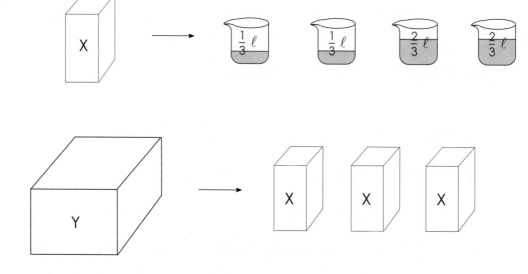

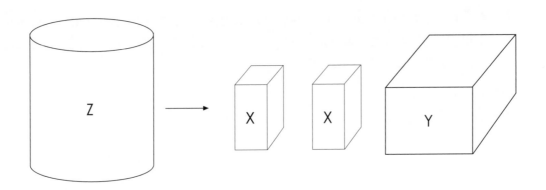

(a) Container X contains _____ liter(s) of water.

(b) Container Z contains _____ liter(s) of water more than Container Y.

(c) Container Y and Container Z together contain _____ liter(s) of water less than 10 Container X.

(d) To fill four Container Z, I need _____ liter(s) of water.

WORD PROBLEMS

Do these word problems.

1. A barrel contained 30 liters of fruit punch. At a party, some guests drank 18 liters of fruit punch and a waiter spilled 3 liters of it. How much fruit punch was left in the barrel?

2. A bucket contains 15 liters of water when full. A basin contains 3 liters of water when full. How much more water can 6 basins contain than a bucket?

3. Cher's jug has 8 liters of orange juice. Cher has 2 liters of orange juice left in the jug after she has filled up 3 bottles. How many liters of orange juice are in each bottle?

4. Mrs. Lindy made 25 pints of jam She gave 7 pints to her friend and shared the rest among 3 neighbors. How much jam did each neighbor get?

5. Five cans of white paint and four cans of red paint are mixed together to get pink paint. Each can contains 5 gallons of paint. How much pink paint is there?

6. A restaurant prepares 81 cups of lemonade. It sells 72 cups of the drink in one-cup small size glasses and the rest in three-cup large size glasses.
   (a) How many cups of lemonade are put in three-cup glasses?
   (b) If the restaurant sells each three-cup glass of the drink for $2, how much money will it collect from selling all the three-cup glasses?

7. A large fish tank can contain 299 liters of water. Ana fills it with 228 liters of water. She then pours eight 2-liter buckets of water into the tank.
   (a) How much water is there in the tank now?
   (b) How much more water can the tank hold?

8. Father's car has a gas tank which can contain 16 gallons of gas. He used 2 gallons of gas on Monday. On Tuesday, he used 9 gallons of gas. On Wednesday, he went to the gas station to top up his gas to a full tank.
   (a) How many gallons of gas did Father use on Monday and Tuesday together?
   (b) If he had 2 gallons of gas left, how many gallons of gas would he need to top up to get a full tank?

Take the Challenge!

1. Container A contains 2 gallons more water than Container B. Container C contains 2 gallons less water than Container A. Container D contains 2 gallons more water than Container A.
    (a) Which 2 containers contain the same amount of water?
    (b) How much more water can Container D contain than Container B?

2. Tank D is filled with 4 times as much water as Tank A. Tank A is filled with 4 liters more water than Tank B. Tank B and Tank C together are filled with as much water as Tank D.
    If Tank D is filled with 28 liters of water, how much water is in Tank C?

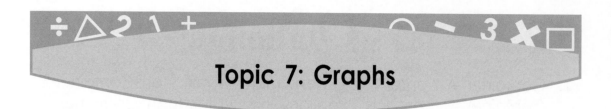
1. Count the number of each type of flower and creature in the garden. Then color the graph to show the number of each type of flower and creature you have counted.
   Use a different color for each item.

Number of flowers and creatures in the garden

	Daffodil	Rose	Daisy	Butterfly	Bee	Snail

Row labels: 8, 7, 6, 5, 4, 3, 2, 1

2. Count the number of each type of vehicle shown below.
   Then color the graph to show the number of each type of vehicle
   you have counted.
   Use a different color for each type of vehicle.

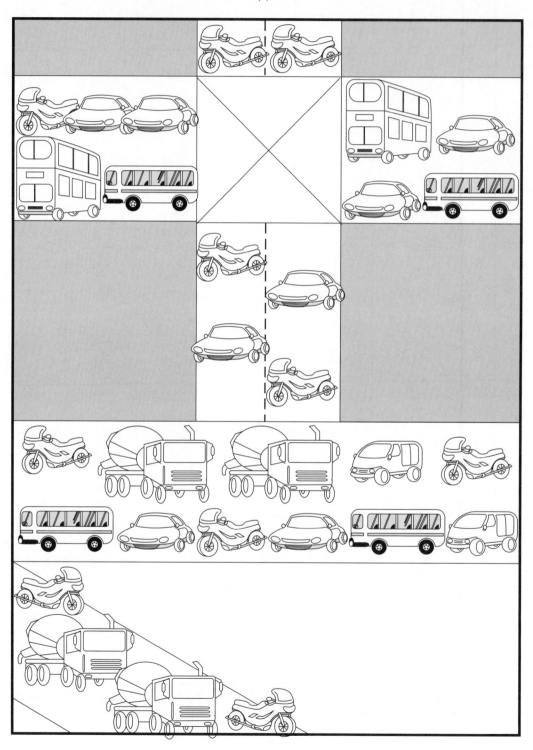

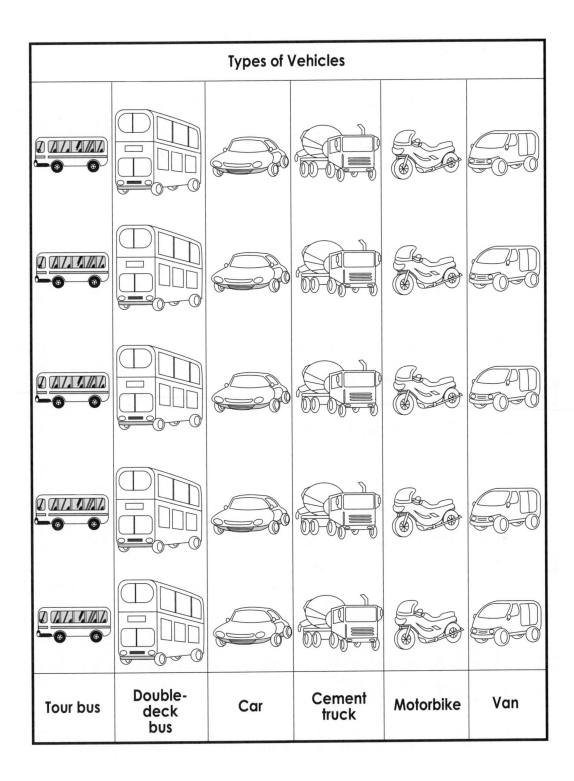

Types of Vehicles					
Tour bus	Double-deck bus	Car	Cement truck	Motorbike	Van

Each vehicle symbol stands for 2 vehicles.

Fill in the blanks.

3. If 🍃 stands for 2 leaves, 🍃 🍃 🍃 🍃 stand for _____ leaves.

4. If 👧 stands for 3 girls, 👧 👧 👧 👧 👧 👧 stand for _____ girls.

5. Each ⬜ stands for 4 boxes, so ⬜ ⬜ ⬜ ⬜ ⬜ stand for _____ boxes.

6. Each 🧁 stands for 5 cupcakes, so 🧁 🧁 🧁 🧁 🧁 🧁 🧁 stand for _____ cupcakes.

7. Each 🐟 represents 10 fish, 🐟 🐟 🐟 🐟 🐟 🐟 🐟 represent _____ fish.

8. If 🐢 🐢 🐢 represent 9 terrapins, 30 terrapins are represented by _____ 🐢 .

9. If ✏ ✏ ✏ ✏ ✏ represent 20 pencils, 8 pencils are represented by _____ ✏ .

10. If $ $ $ $ represent 40 dollars, 90 dollars are represented by _____ $.

11. If ✓ ✓ ✓ represent 12 points, 28 points are represented by _____ ✓ .

12. If 🕐 🕐 🕐 🕐 🕐 represent 25 clocks, 40 clocks are represented by _____ 🕐 .

13. The picture graph below shows the number of pairs of shoes each child has. Study it and fill in the blanks below.

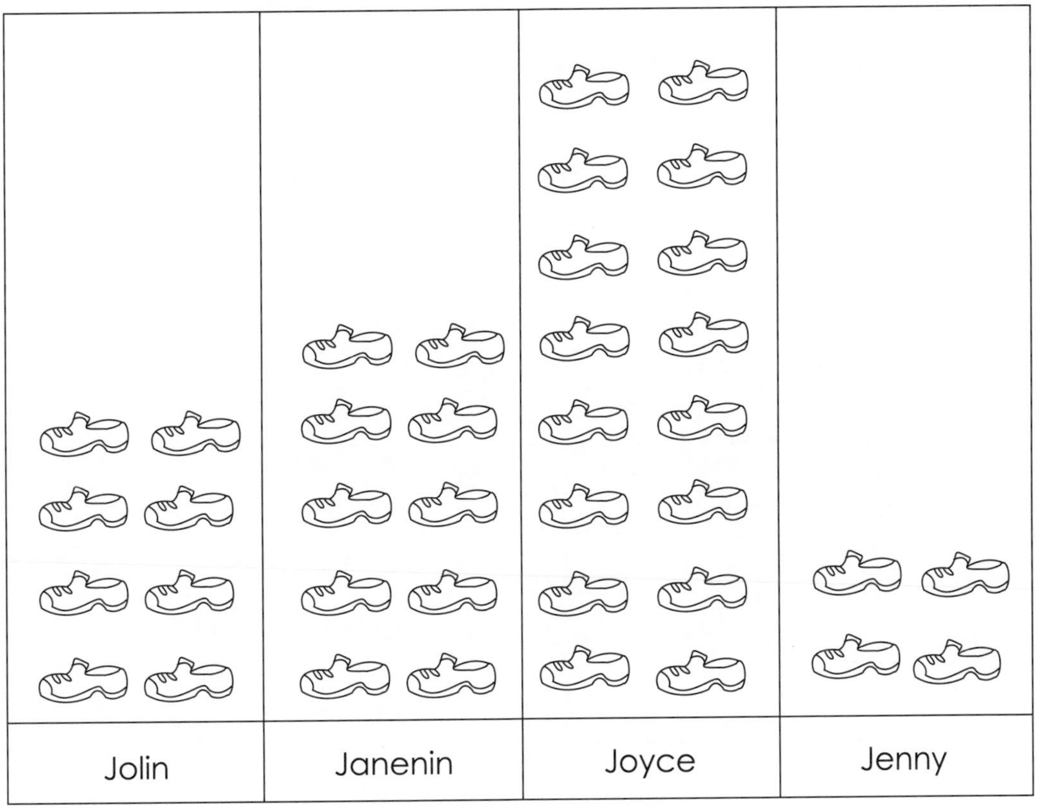

| Jolin | Janenin | Joyce | Jenny |

Each  👟👟 represents 1 pair of shoes.

(a) _____ has the most number of pairs of shoes.

(b) _____ has 1 fewer pair of shoes than Janenin.

(c) Jenny has 2 fewer pairs of shoes than _____.

(d) Joyce has _____ pairs of shoes more than Jenny.

(e) Altogether, the girls have _____ pairs of shoes.

14. The picture graph below shows the ages of 5 women. Study it and fill in the blanks below.

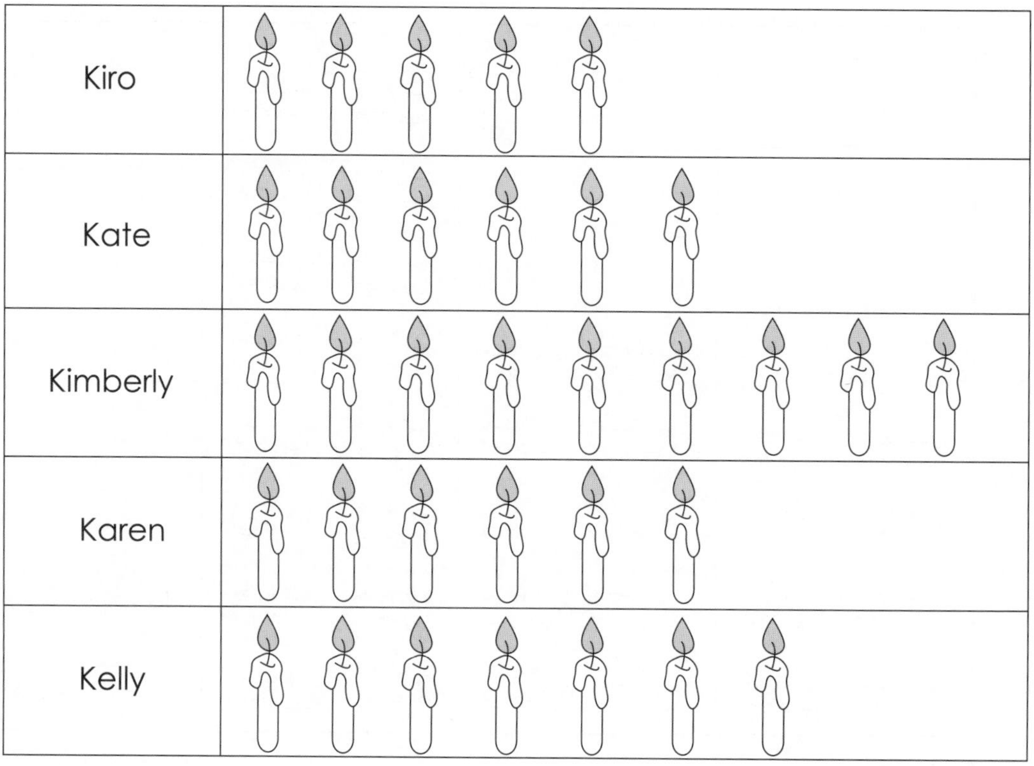

Kiro	
Kate	
Kimberly	
Karen	
Kelly	

Each  ⚪ represents 5 years of age.

(a) _____ is the youngest of the 5 women.

(b) The difference between the ages of Karen and Kiro is _____ years.

(c) _____ and _____ are of the same age.

(d) Kimberly is _____ years older than Karen.

(e) Altogether, the 5 women are _____ years old.

84

15. The picture graph below shows the capacity of five containers. Study it and fill in the blanks below.

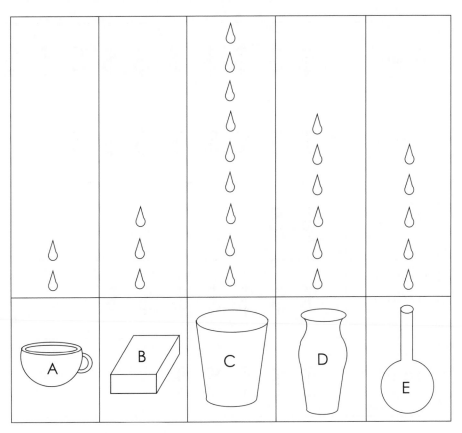

Each 💧 represents 4 pints.

(a) Container _____ can fill 20 pints of water.

(b) Container A can fill _____ pints of water less than Container D.

(c) Container D can fill 3 times as much water as Container _____ .

(d) Container C can fill _____ times as much water as Container B.

(e) Containers C and D together can fill _____ more pints of water than Containers A and B together.

16. The picture graph below shows the amount of money each child saves per month. Study it and fill in the blanks below.

Anita	$ $ $ $ $ $ $ $ $ $
Benson	$ $ $ $ $ $ $ $
Cathy	$ $
Dion	$ $ $ $ $ $ $
Eason	$ $ $ $ $

Each $ represents 10 dollars.

(a) Dion and Eason save _____ dollars altogether.

(b) Anita saves _____ times as many dollars as Cathy.

(c) If Benson spends $$, he will be left with _____ dollars.

(d) If Anita spends $$$$, she will be left with _____ dollars.

(e) The money that Benson, Cathy and Dion save is used to buy a present for their friend, Eason. Eason's present costs _____ dollars.

17. The picture graph below shows the number of letters each child receives. Study it and fill in the blanks below.

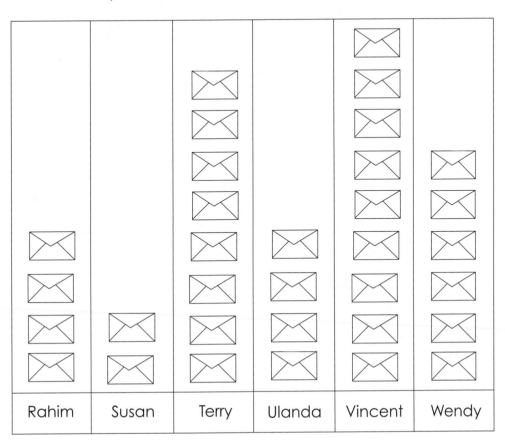

Each ✉ represents 3 letters.

(a) Terry receives _____ times as many letters as Rahim.

(b) Vincent receives _____ more letters than Susan and Ulanda together.

(c) _____ and Susan receives as many letters as Terry.

(d) Rahim receives _____ fewer letters than Vincent and Susan together.

(e) Altogether, the children receive _____ letters.

18. Count the number of marbles each boy has. Then complete the picture graph below.

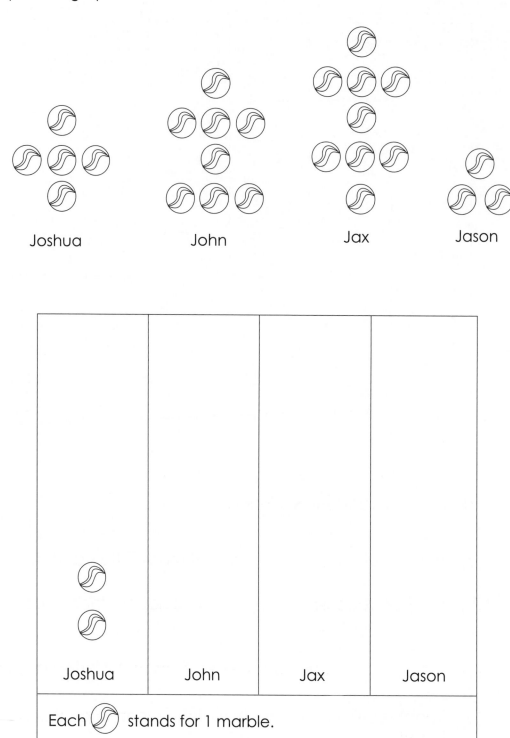

Joshua   John   Jax   Jason

Each ⟳ stands for 1 marble.

19. There are some fruits displayed at a fruit stall for sale. Count the number of each type of fruit. Then complete the picture graph below.

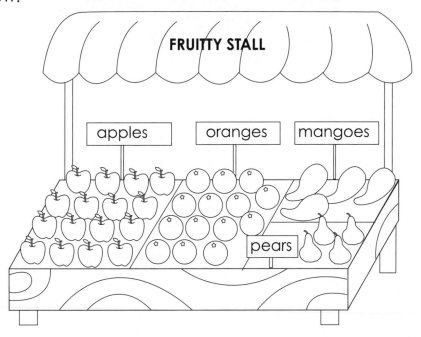

Each △ stands for 2 fruits.			
Apple	Pear	Orange	Mango

20. The table shows the number of flowers each garden has.

Garden	Number of flowers
A	18
B	9
C	6
D	15
E	21

Use  to represent 3 flowers. Complete the picture graph below.

A	B	C	D	E

21. The table shows the number of cookies each child made for a bake sale.

Name	Number of cookies
Carla	20
Laura	15
Kaylie	10
Juan	25
Paul	35

Use ⊗ to represent 5 cookies. Complete the picture graph below.

Carla	Laura	Kaylie	Juan	Paul

22. The scripts show the number of points scored by each student in a math test.

Name: Linda $\frac{80}{100}$

1. _____
2. _____
3. _____
3. _____
4. _____

Name: Fiona $\frac{90}{100}$

1. _____
2. _____
3. _____
4. _____
5. _____

Name: Kim $\frac{100}{100}$

1. _____
2. _____
3. _____
4. _____
5. _____

Name: Ron $\frac{60}{100}$

1. _____
2. _____
3. _____
4. _____
5. _____

Name: Norman $\frac{50}{100}$

1. _____
2. _____
3. _____
4. _____
5. _____

Name: Colin $\frac{70}{100}$

1. _____
2. _____
3. _____
4. _____
5. _____

Use ☆ to represent 10 points. Complete the picture graph below.

Linda	Fiona	Kim	Ron	Norman	Colin

Topic 8: Geometry

1. Write "straight line" or "curved line" under each line.

(a)	(b)
(c)	(d)
(e)	(f)
(g)	(h)
(i)	(j)

2. Count and write the number of straight and curved lines for each figure.

(a) Number of straight lines = _____

Number of curved lines = _____

(b) Number of straight lines = _____

Number of curved lines = _____

(c) Number of straight lines = _____

Number of curved lines = _____

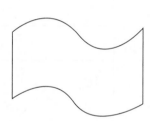

(d) Number of straight lines = _____

Number of curved lines = _____

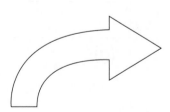

(e) Number of straight lines = _____

Number of curved lines = _____

3. Join each shaded shape with the word that describes it.

(a)

Circle

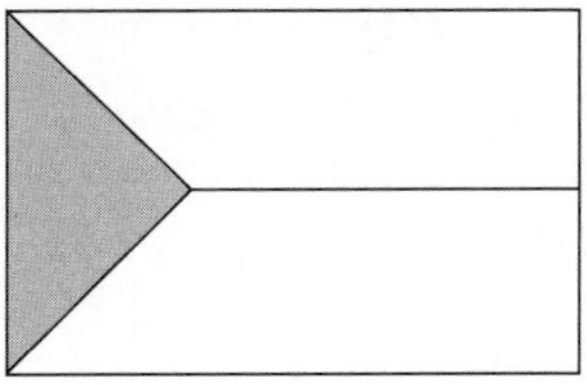

(b)

Square

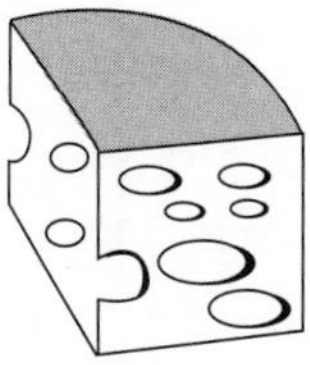

(c)

Half circle

(d)

Rectangle

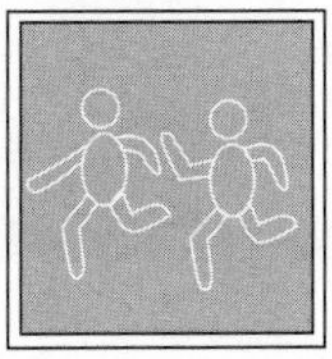

(e)

Triangle

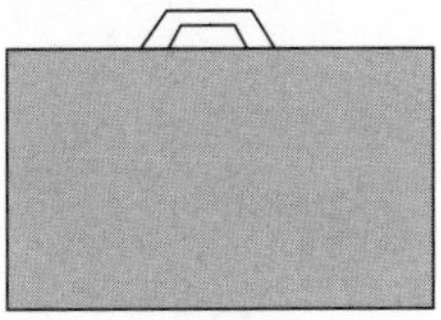

(f)

Quarter circle

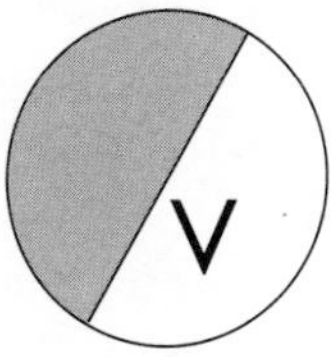

4. Name the shape which is shaded.

(a)

_____

(b)

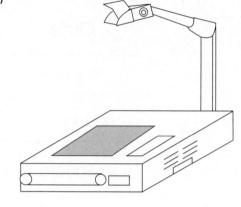

_____

(c)

_____

(d)

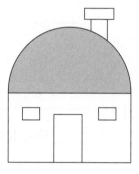

_____

(e)

_____

(f)

_____

5. Study the diagram. Then fill in the blanks.

(a)

There are _____ ovals, _____ rectangles, _____

triangles, _____ circles and _____ squares.

(b)

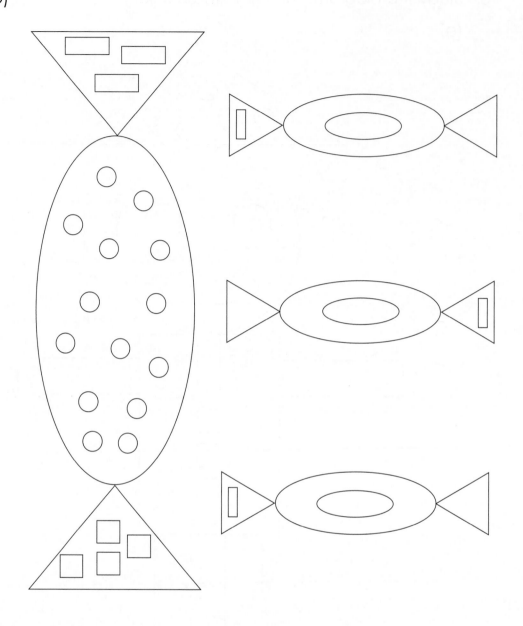

There are _____ ovals, _____ rectangles, _____

triangles, _____ half circles, _____ circles and _____

squares.

(c)

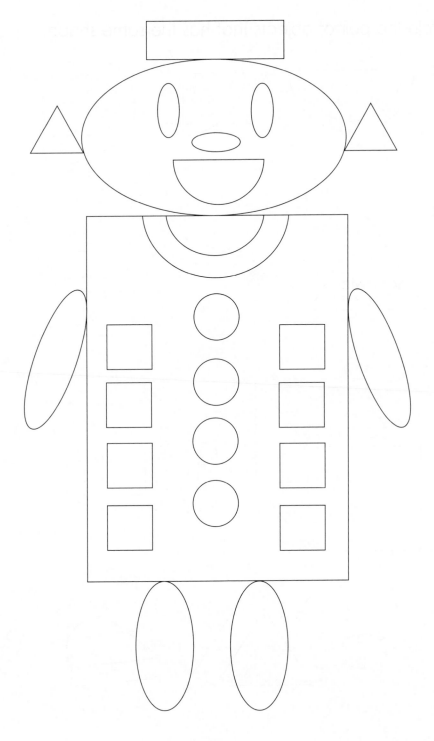

There are _____ ovals, _____ rectangles, _____ triangles, _____ half circles, _____ circles and _____ squares.

6. Circle the pair of objects that has the same shape.

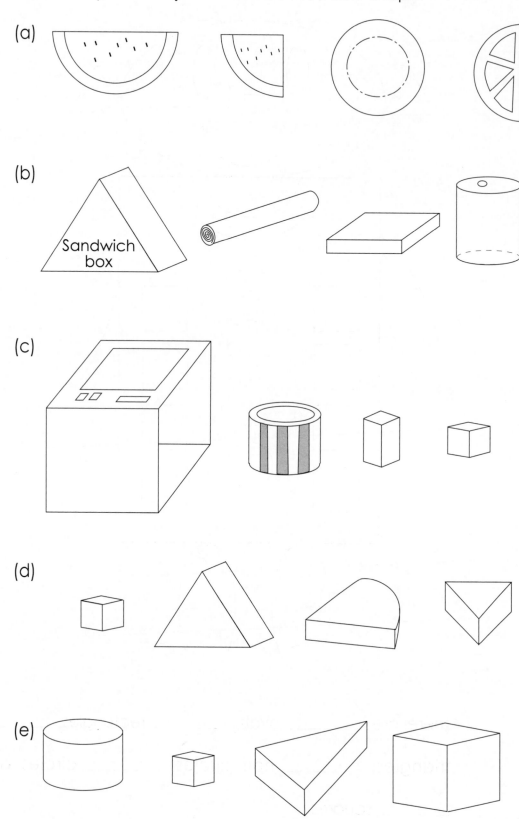

(a)

(b)

Sandwich box

(c)

(d)

(e)

7. Study the solids below and fill in the blanks.

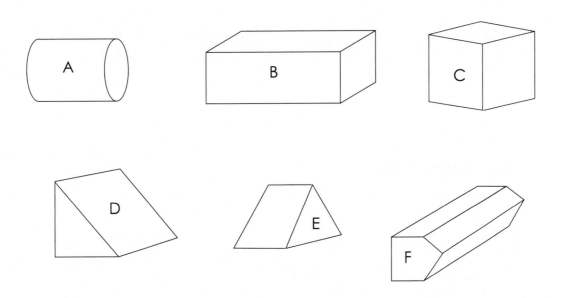

(a) Solid A has _____ flat faces and _____ curved face(s).

(b) Solid B has _____ flat faces and _____ curved face(s).

(c) _____ faces of Solid C are squares.

(d) Solid D has _____ faces.

(e) _____ faces of Solid D are triangles.

(f) Solid E has _____ faces.

(g) Three faces of Solid E are _____.

(h) Solid F has _____ faces.

(i) _____ faces of Solid F are rectangles.

(j) Solid _____ is the only object with a curved face.

8. Circle two parts to form the required shape.

(a) A circle

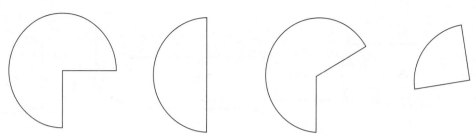

(b) A rectangle

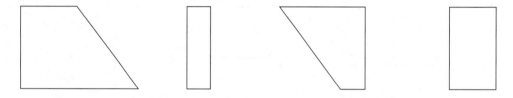

(c) A square

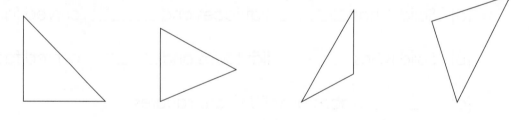

(d) A triangle

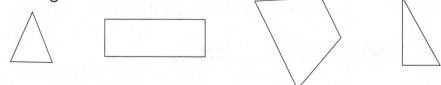

(e) A pentagon (5-sided figure with equal sides)

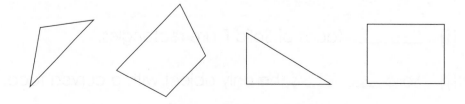

9. Draw lines on each figure to show how it is formed by the given shapes.

(a) 5 triangles

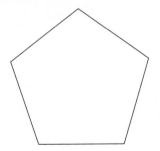

(b) 6 triangles

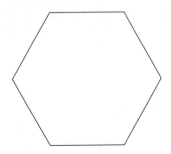

(c) 1 square and 4 rectangles

(d) 2 triangles and 1 rectangle

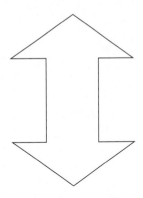

(e) 1 half circle and 1 rectangle

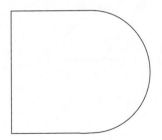

(f) 1 square, 1 triangle and 1 rectangle

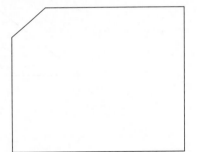

Take the Challenge!

1. How many ways can a rectangle be divided into two equal parts?

2. How many ways can a square be divided into four equal parts?

3. Count the number of triangles you can find in the diagram below.

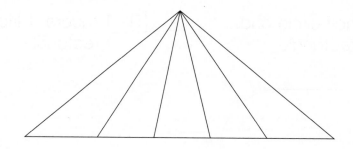

Topic 9: Shapes and Patterns

1. Study the pattern. Then circle the shape that comes next.

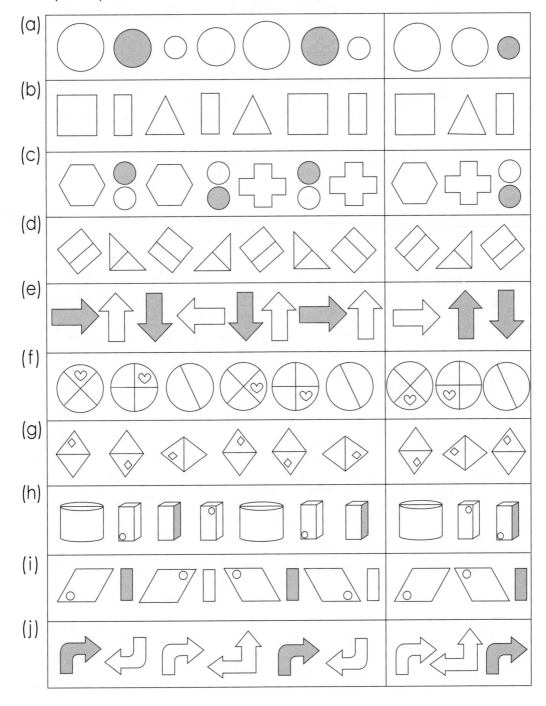

2. Study the pattern. Then draw the shape that comes next.

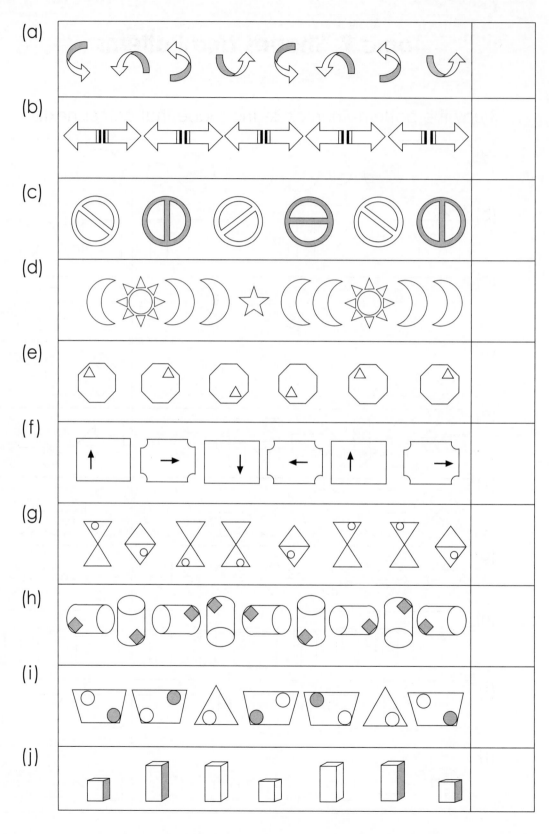

3. Study the pattern. Then draw the missing shapes in the blanks.

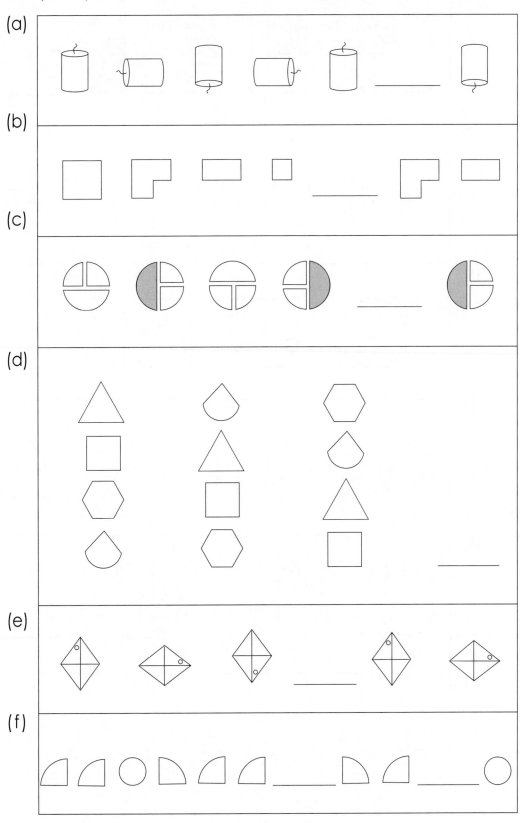

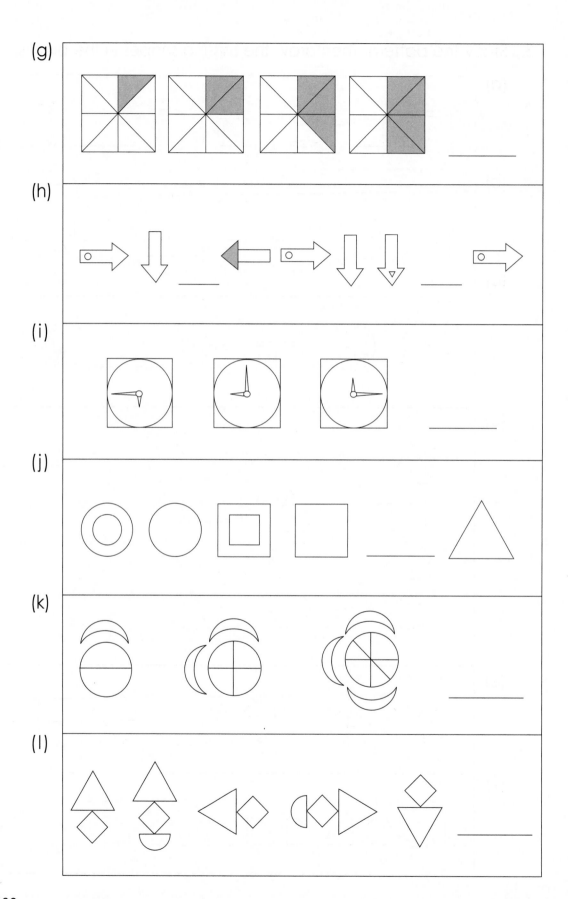

(g)

(h)

(i)

(j)

(k)

(l)

108

Take the Challenge!

1. Draw the missing figures or shapes in the boxes to make the patterns complete.

(a)

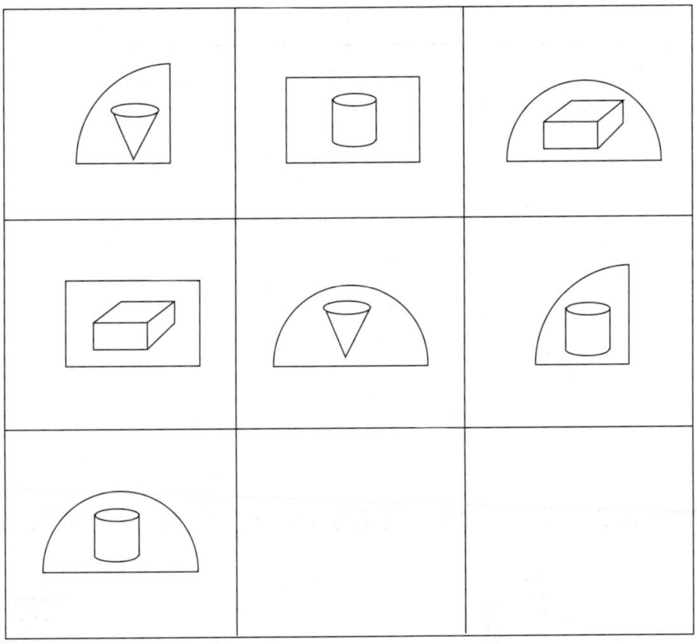

(b)

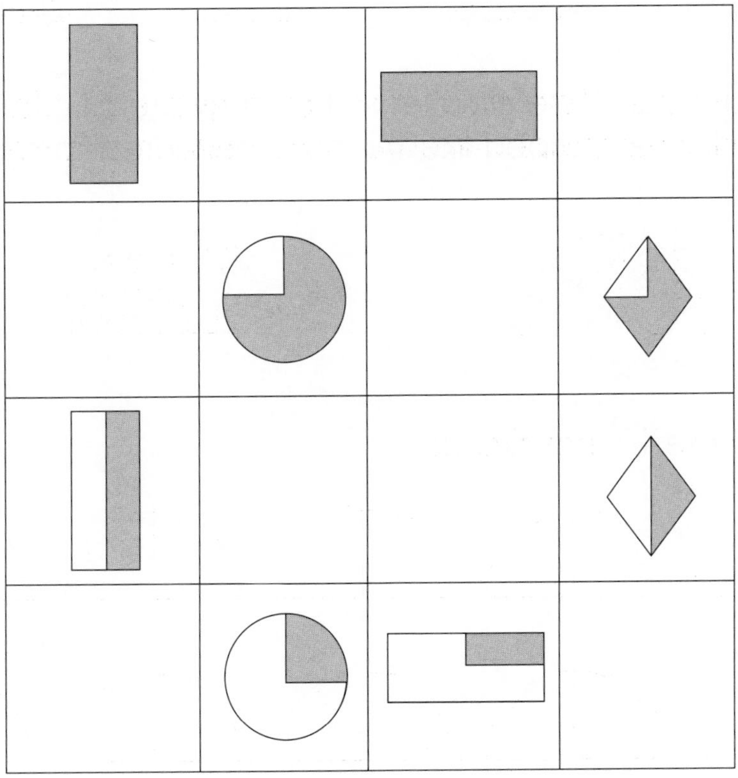

2. How many triangles are there in this figure?

3. Each quarter circle must be shaded in one of the following ways:

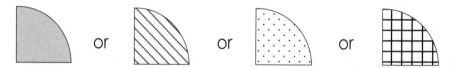

Can you shade 10 semicircles so that they are all different? Note that semicircles shaped like this are considered to be the same type:

Shade these 10 semicircles:

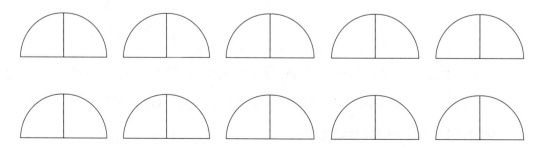

End-Of-Year Review

PART 1

Fill in the correct answers.

1. 896 is 434 and _____ .

2. 248 is 42 less than _____ tens.

3. In the number 375, the difference between the values of the digits 3 and 5 is _____ .

4.
   ```
      3  ♡
   +  ♡  8
   ─────────
      8  2
   ```

   Each ♡ has the same value. The value of each ♡ is _____ .

5. The table shows the number of visitors at the zoo on Saturday and Sunday.

Day	Number of visitors
Saturday	506
Sunday	329

   (a) _____ more people visited the zoo on Saturday than on Sunday.

   (b) _____ people visited the zoo on the 2 days.

6. Leon has 18 marbles while Frank has 6 marbles. Leon must give _____ marbles to Frank so that both of them will have the same number of marbles.

7. Maria has 400 stickers. 85 of them are yellow, 121 are green and the rest are blue. She has _____ more blue stickers than yellow ones.

8. Six cups of water will fill a jug. Two cups of water will fill a mug.

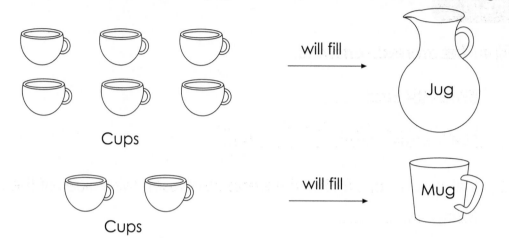

Cups   will fill
                                                        —————→   Jug

Cups   will fill
                                                        —————→   Mug

_____ mugs will fill the jug.

9. 5 × _____ = 400 − 365

10. _____ ÷ 2 = 80 ÷ 10

11. _____ fives = 50 = _____ tens

12. _____ × 4 = 19 + 17

13. If ☆ × ☆ = 16, then the value of ☆ is _____.

14. 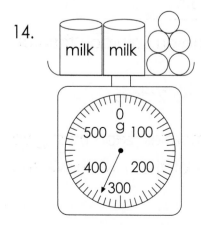 If each can of milk weighs 140 g, then each ball weighs _____ g.

15. Study these pictures and answer the questions.

    (a) Which object is the lightest, A, B or C? _____

    (b) Which object is the heaviest, A, B or C? _____

16. Fill in the blanks with "in.", "ft", "yd", "oz" or "lb".

    (a) My teacher's height is about 6 _____.

    (b) I bake a cake that weighs about 1 _____.

    (c) A whiteboard marker is about 5 _____ long.

    (d) Pat used 9 _____ of flour to make some pies.

17. Draw a line 5 cm shorter than 11 cm. Start at the given dot.

    •

18. Measure all the 3 sides of this triangle.

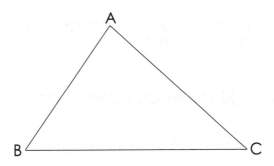

    (a) AB = _____ cm

    (b) AC = _____ cm

    (c) BC = _____ cm

    (d) The total length of all the 3 sides is _____ cm.

19. Study these diagrams.

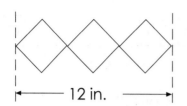 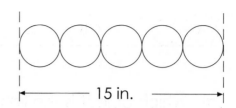

Find the length of RS.

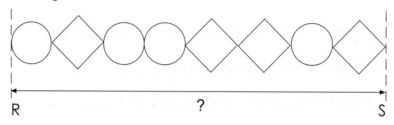

R   ?   S

The length of RS is _____ in.

20. Look at these pictures. Then answer the questions below.

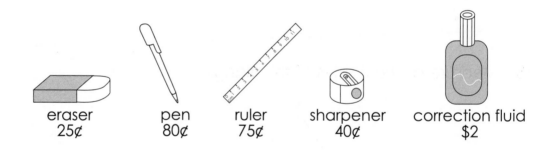

eraser 25¢   pen 80¢   ruler 75¢   sharpener 40¢   correction fluid $2

(a) I have exactly $1.00. Which 2 items can I buy?

_____ and _____

(b) The cost of a pen is the same as the cost of 2 _____.

(c) The correction fluid is _____ cents more expensive than the eraser.

(d) A sharpener and a ruler cost $ _____ altogether.

21. $4.25 = _____ cents

22. 438 cents = $_____

23. $3.50 = _____ quarters.

24. Write this amount in numbers:
Six hundred thirteen dollars and two cents. _____

25. Fill in the missing number.

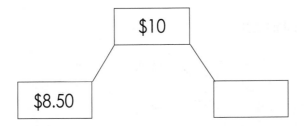

26. Count the total amount of money in the purse.

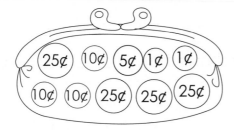

$_____

27. Arrange these fractions in order. Begin with the smallest.

$\frac{1}{8}$ $\frac{1}{10}$ $\frac{1}{3}$ $\frac{1}{2}$ $\frac{1}{7}$

_____

28. What fraction of the figure is *not* shaded?

_____ of the figure is not shaded.

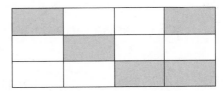

29. Fill in the missing fraction.

$\frac{3}{11}$, $\frac{2}{11}$ and ☐ make 1 whole.

30. There are _____ quarters in 6 wholes.

31. Circle $\frac{2}{3}$ of these objects.

32.  The clock shows that it is _____ minutes to 4.

33.  This clock is 25 minutes fast. The correct time is

_____ .

34. 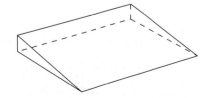   (a) This solid has _____ faces.
    (b) How many faces are rectangles?

_____

35.  This figure is made up of a _____ , a

_____ and a _____ .

36. 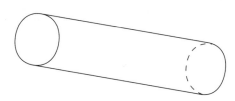 (a) This solid has _____ faces.

(b) How many face(s) are curved?

_____

37. The graph shows the amount of money 4 girls saved in one month. Study this picture graph. Then answer the questions below.

(a) Lynn saved $ _____ more than Kim in 1 month.

(b) Lynn saved twice the amount _____ saved in 1 month.

(c) Jean will save $100 in _____ months if she saves the same amount every month.

(d) The 4 girls saved $ _____ altogether in 1 month.

38. Draw the pattern that comes next.

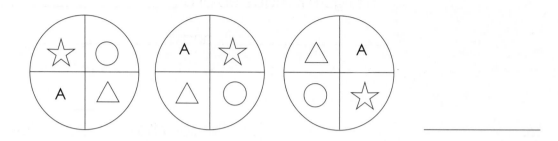

_____

39. Study the pattern. Find the missing numbers.

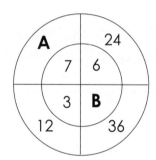

A = _____

B = _____

40. Each bottle contains $\frac{1}{2}$ ℓ of water. The water in 6 such bottles is poured into an empty fish tank. How much water is in the fish tank?

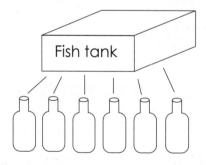

The fish tank has _____ liters of water.

PART 2

Solve these problems. Show your work clearly.

41. Mrs. Armando paid $19 for 2 bottles of detergent and 1 bottle of floor cleaner. If the bottle of floor cleaner cost $5, what was the cost of 1 bottle of detergent?

Answer: _____

42. 379 girls and 436 boys were enrolled in a school. 88 moved away. How many children are now enrolled?

Answer: _____

43. A box of crayons weighs 540 g. An empty box weighs 189 g. What is the weight of the crayons in the box?

Answer: _____

44. There were 6 men on a bus. There were 4 times as many women as there were men on the bus. How many women were there on the bus?

Answer: _____

45. Keith has 5 quarters, 6 dimes and 3 nickels. He wants to buy a chicken burger that costs $2.95. How much more money does he need?

$2.95

Answer: _____

46. Allie cut a pizza into 8 equal pieces. She and her 2 cousins each ate 2 pieces of the pizza. What fraction of the pizza was left?

Answer: _____

47. A piece of fabric is 31 yd long. A tailor uses 3 yd of it and cuts the remaining fabric into 4 equal pieces. What is the length of each of these 4 pieces of fabric?

Answer: _____

48. A bag of tomatoes cost $8. There were 10 tomatoes in each bag. Mrs. Ong bought 40 tomatoes.
(a) How many bags did she buy?
(b) How much did she pay for the tomatoes?

Answer: (a) _____

(b) _____

49. Nicholas has 88 fewer stamps than Osman. If Nicholas has 140 stamps, how many stamps do the 2 boys have altogether?

Answer: _____

50. Kimberly bought 5 pencils. Each pencil cost 25 cents. How much change did Kimberly get when she gave $2 to the cashier?

Answer: _____

1. Yanni made 100 paper flowers. She first made 2 red paper flowers, then 3 yellow ones and finally 5 green ones. She then repeated this order of making the flowers until she made all 100 of them.
   (a) How many yellow flowers were made altogether?
   (b) What is the color of the 87th flower made?

2. Two blocks of school building are 100 meters apart. Trees are to be planted between the two blocks in a straight line such that the trees are either 10 meters away from the blocks or 10 meters away from one another. How many trees are there?

3. Observe the pattern and fill in the correct shapes in the last diagram.

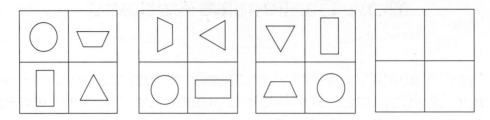

4. Fill in the numbers 2, 3, 4, 5, 6 and 7 in the small circles such that the multiplication of the three numbers on the small ring is the same as the sum of the five numbers on the big ring.

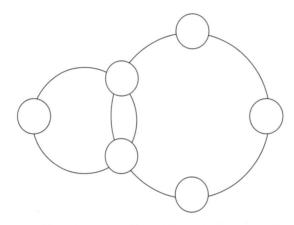

5. Ken read a story book which had 100 pages. He read 80 pages on the first day. On the second day, he read half of the remaining pages and 5 more pages. How many more pages did Ken need to read to finish the book?

6. From the nine numbers 0, 1, 2, 3, 4, 5, 6, 7 and 8, choose eight different numbers to fill in the boxes. Each box can be filled by one number only.

    $$\boxed{} + \boxed{} = \boxed{}\boxed{}$$

    $$\boxed{} \times \boxed{} = \boxed{}\boxed{}$$

7. Do the following by mental calculation.

    $$98 + 101 + 102 + 96 + 106 + 99 + 100$$

8. In each of the following, the digits are being covered by small pieces of paper. What is the sum of all the digits covered?

    (a)

    $$- \qquad\qquad\qquad\qquad 1$$

    Sum of all the digits covered = _____

    (b)

    $$\boxed{}\boxed{}$$

    $$+ \quad \boxed{}\boxed{}$$

    $$\overline{\qquad 1 \quad 4 \quad 9 \qquad}$$

    Sum of all the digits covered = _____

9. Find the value of
   $20 - 19 + 18 - 17 + 16 - 15 + 14 - 13 + 12 - 11 + 10 - 9 + 8 - 7 + 6 - 5 + 4 - 3 + 2 - 1$.

10. For each of the following, fill in the boxes with the numbers 10, 11, 12 and 13. Each number can be used only once in each sentence.

    □ + □ − □ = □

    □ − □ + □ = □

11. Angie has one nickel, one dime and one quarter in her purse. How many different amount of money can she make using one, two or all the three coins? List the different amount of money by drawing.

12. From the following diagrams, find the weight of one ◯ and one ▮ . One ⬤ weighs 12 g.

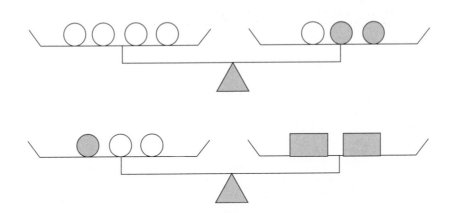

◯ = _____ g, ▮ = _____ g

13. In each of the following, each shape represents a number. Can you find the numbers?

(a) ☐ + ☐ + △ + △ = 18

☐ + ☐ + △ + △ + △ + △ = 24

☐ = _____ , △ = _____ .

(b) $\bigcirc = \triangledown + \triangledown + \triangledown + \triangledown + \triangledown$

$\bigcirc \times \triangledown = 20$

$\bigcirc = $ _____ , $\triangledown = $ _____ .

14. Some men are planting 18 trees in a park. The trees are to be planted in a straight line at equal distances apart. If the 1st tree and the 6th tree are 10 meters apart, what is the distance covered by the 18 trees?

15. Observe each of the following patterns and complete the missing diagram in the box.

(a)

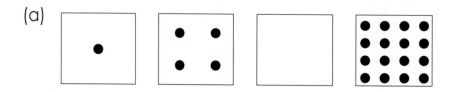

(b)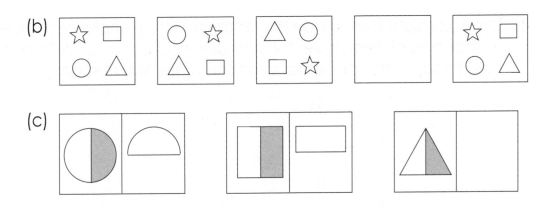

(c)

16. Some black and white beads are arranged in a certain order as shown.

(a)

What is the color of the 22nd bead and the 28th bead?

The 22nd bead is _____ in color.

The 28th bead is _____ in color.

(b)

What is the color of the 34th bead and the 51st bead?

The 34th bead is _____ in color.

The 51st bead is _____ in color.

17. There are 5 squares formed by straws in this figure (4 small squares and 1 big square). Can you rearrange 3 straws to form 3 squares of equal size? Draw the new arrangement below.

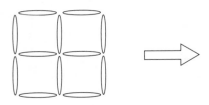

18. Using 3 straight lines, divide this rectangle into 6 smaller rectangles so that in each rectangle, the numbers add up to 18. (A line may pass through the space between the digits of a number.)

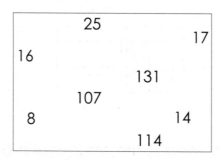

19. If the secret code for the number 382 is 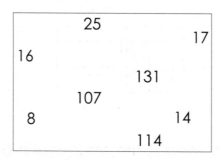, what number does each of the following codes stand for?

(a) stands for the number _____.

(b) stands for the number _____.

20. A pizza is cut into 3 pieces X, Y and Z.

X is $\frac{1}{2}$ of the pizza.

Y is $\frac{1}{3}$ of the pizza.

What fraction of the pizza is Z?

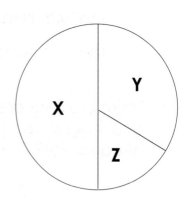

21. Solve the following problem using a quick and easy method.

$14 + 12 + 16 + 18 + 18 + 16 + 12 + 14 + 14 + 12 + 16 + 18 =$ _____

22.

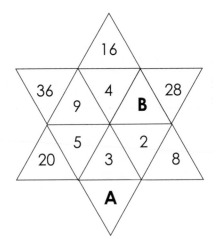

Study the patterns in the star.
Find the values of A and B.

A = _____

B = _____

23. Anthony is taller than Bobby.
Clive is shorter than David.
Anthony is shorter than Clive.
Their heights are 64 in., 60 in., 57 in. and 51 in. (from tallest to shortest). Can you name the boy by the given height? Write the answers in the table below.

Height	Name of Boy
64 in.	
60 in.	
57 in.	
51 in.	

24. How many kittens are there if the kittens together have 6 more legs than ears? There are not more than 5 kittens. Guess and check your answer by using the table below to help you.

Number of kittens	Number of ears	Number of legs	How many more legs than ears?

Answers

Topic 1: Addition and Subtraction (Mental Calculation)

1. (a) 59, +20, 59
   (b) 79, +30, 75, +4, 79
   (c) 155, +40, 152, +3, 155
   (d) 147, +20, 143, +4, 147
   (e) 290, +40, 285, +5, 290
   (f) 93   (g) 78   (h) 95
   (i) 91   (j) 86   (k) 121
   (l) 141 (m) 151 (n) 326
   (o) 499 (p) 191 (q) 282
   (r) 382 (s) 492 (t) 541
2. (a) 222   (b) 525, 525, 625
   (c) 243, 3, 100, 243 + 100 = 343
   (d) 341, 4, 100, 341 + 100 = 441
   (e) 413, 5, 100, 413 + 100 = 513
   (f) 151 + 100 = 251 (g) 244 + 100 = 344
   (h) 707 + 100 = 807 (i) 860 + 100 = 960
   (j) 662 + 100 = 762 (k) 542 + 100 = 642
   (l) 332 + 100 = 432 (m) 421 + 100 = 521
   (n) 301 + 100 = 401 (o) 227 + 100 = 327
   (p) 465 + 100 = 565 (q) 763 + 100 = 863
   (r) 685 + 100 = 785 (s) 410 + 100 = 510
   (t) 518 + 100 = 618
3. (a) 25, −20, 28, −3, 25
   (b) 32, −50, 39, −7, 32
   (c) 222, −20, 225, −3, 222
   (d) 659, −10, 668, −9, 659
   (e) 525, −40, 527, −2, 525
   (f) 154   (g) 111   (h) 232
   (i) 331   (j) 421   (k) 511
   (l) 599   (m) 750   (n) 828
   (o) 954   (p) 219   (q) 327
   (r) 415   (s) 504   (t) 618
4. (a) 234, 1, 1, 234
   (b) 325 + 2 = 327; 100 − 98 = 2;
       325 + 2 = 327
   (c) 265 + 3 = 268; 100 − 97 = 3;
       265 + 3 = 268
   (d) 423 + 4 = 427; 100 − 96 = 4;
       423 + 4 = 427
   (e) 516 + 5 = 521; 100 − 95 = 5;
       516 + 5 = 521
   (f) 147   (g) 821   (h) 527
   (i) 459   (j) 622   (k) 334
   (l) 221   (m) 77   (n) 256
   (o) 327   (p) 420   (q) 168
   (r) 15   (s) 233   (t) 369

5. 186, 261, 216, 327, 235, 251, 152, 171, 75,
   285, 188, 236, 215, 326, 228, 248, 149, 80
6. (a) 433   (b) 370   (c) 714
   (d) 511   (e) 239   (f) 116
   (g) 452   (h) 357   (i) 211
   (j) 11   (k) 576   (l) 374
   (m) 640   (n) 220
7. 139   8. 512   9. 280
10. 940   11. 770   12. 350

Word Problems

1. $87 \xrightarrow{-10} 77 \xrightarrow{-8} 69$
2. (a) $23 \xrightarrow{+40} 63 \xrightarrow{+8} 71$
   (b) 71 + 20 = 91
3. (a) 99 + 98 = 97 + 100 = 197
   (b) 240 − 197 = 43
4. (a) 126 − 99 = 26 + 1 = 27
   (b) 99 − 23 = 76
5. (a) $82 \xrightarrow{-20} 62 \xrightarrow{-6} 56$
   (b) $56 \xrightarrow{+50} 106 \xrightarrow{+6} 112$
6. (a) 125 − 97 = 25 + 3 = 28
   (b) 18 + 97 = 15 + 100 = 115

Take the Challenge!

1. (a)
36	146	17
52	99	22
120	16	117

   (b)
90	81	111
79	98	59
97	66	95

   (c)
111	101	99
116	321	221
97	100	68

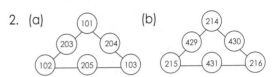

2. (a) 101, 203, 204, 102, 205, 103
   (b) 214, 429, 430, 215, 431, 216

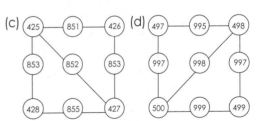

   (c) 425, 851, 426, 853, 852, 853, 428, 855, 427
   (d) 497, 995, 498, 997, 998, 997, 500, 999, 499

[It is interesting to note:
(sum of the three given numbers in a triangle) ÷ 2 – (any given number) = the missing end number opposite this given number.]

3. There are many possible ways of filling in the numbers. The answer for each part shown below is just one way.

(a)

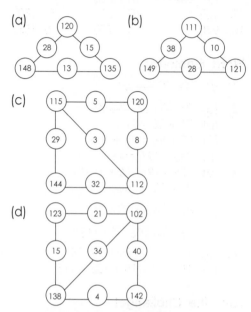

(b)

(c)

(d)

Topic 2: Multiplication Tables and Division of 4, 5 and 10

1.

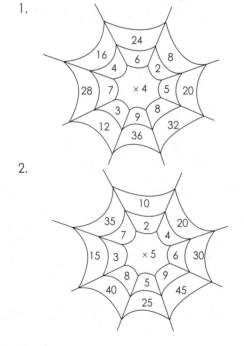

2.

3.

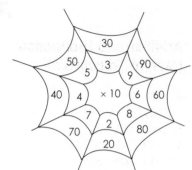

4. (a) 4, 12   (b) 5, 20   (c) 10, 20
   (d) 4, 36   (e) 10, 60   (f) 5, 35
5. 24, 6
6. 35, 7
7. 30, 3
8. 10
9. 8
10. 5
11. 4
12. 5
13. (a) 10   (b) 6   (c) 8
    (d) 45   (e) 8   (f) 36
    (g) 9   (h) 3   (i) 24
    (j) 12
14. 20, 10, 40, 8, 4, 20, 5, 30, 10, 50, 5
15. (a) 4   (b) 9   (c) tens
    (d) 7   (e) 5   (f) 5
    (g) 4   (h) 10   (i) 1
    (j) 10   (k) 32   (l) 25
    (m) 40   (n) 25   (o) 3

Word Problems

1. (a) 30   (b) 10
2. (a) 9   (b) 7
3. (a) 32   (b) 8
4. (a) 4   (b) 5
5. (a) 10   (b) 50
6. (a) 20   (b) No; 6
7. (a) 40   (b) 8
   (c) 32
8. (a) 45   (b) 5

Take the Challenge!

1. (a) $4 \times \triangle = 24$ (b) $10 \times \square = 70$
        $\triangle = 6$ $\square = 7$

2. Possible answers:
   2 ducks, 12 goats; 4 ducks, 11 goats;
   6 ducks, 10 goats; 8 ducks, 9 goats;

134

10 ducks, 8 goats; 12 ducks, 7 goats;
14 ducks, 6 goats; 16 ducks, 5 goats;
18 ducks, 4 goats; 20 ducks, 3 goats;
22 ducks, 2 goats; 24 ducks, 1 goat

Topic 3: Money

1. (a) $1.11   (b) 990¢   (c) 220¢
   (d) $1.40   (e) $4.25   (f) 99¢
   (g) $2.01   (h) 812¢   (i) $6.15
   (j) 607¢
2. (a) 0.23   (b) 4.70   (c) 9.14
   (d) 1.05   (e) 0.15   (f) 1.25
3. (a) 75   (b) 92   (c) 5
   (d) 270   (e) 572   (f) 345
4. (a) 2, 5   (b) 27, 0   (c) 38, 2
   (d) 6, 15   (e) 8, 2   (f) 6, 0
5. (a)

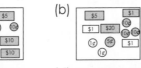

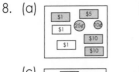

(b)

(c)

(d)

(e)

6. (a) $99.19   (b) $34.05   (c) $1.22
   (d) $81.40   (e) $62.01
7. (a) 2.56   (b) 0.22   (c) 13.10
   (d) 56.50   (e) 11.60   (f) 57.15
   (g) 11.07   (h) 51.55   (i) 62.05
   (j) 56
8. (a)   (b)

(c)   (d)

(e)   (f)

9. (a) 5.50, 5.80   (b) 3.40, 3.90
   (c) 8.60, 8.90   (d) 6.45, 9.45
   (e) 5.95, 7.95   (f) 1.80, 5.80
   (g) 7.30, 7.35   (h) 6.01, 7.00
   (i) 3.90, 6.90   (j) 4.03, 7.03
   (k) 2.85, 2.35   (l) 3.60, 2.95
   (m) 1.56, 0.57   (n) 9.00, 8.93
   (o) 70.00   (p) 90.11

Word Problems

1. (a) $35.15   (b) $0.85
2. (a) $655   (b) $1000
3. (a) $29   (b) $11
4. (a) $32
   (b) Daisy had more savings, $12
5. (a) $272   (b) $38
6. (a) 5   (b) $1.55
7. (a) $150   (b) $111
8. (a) $7.95   (b) $7.95
   (c) $14.95

Take the Challenge!

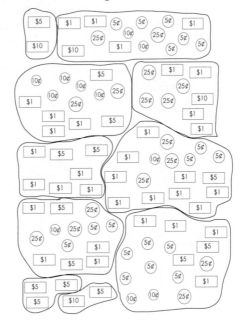

Topic 4: Fractions

1. Check: (a), (c), (e), (f), (h), (i), (j), (l)
2. Check: (b), (e), (h), (i), (j), (l)

3. (a) $\frac{3}{8}$ (b) $\frac{3}{8}$ (c) $\frac{1}{2}$ (d) $\frac{5}{12}$

    (e) $\frac{1}{4}$ (f) $\frac{1}{2}$ (g) $\frac{2}{10}$ (h) $\frac{2}{4}$

    (i) $\frac{5}{8}$ (j) $\frac{2}{4}$ (k) $\frac{5}{9}$ (l) $\frac{5}{12}$

    (m) $\frac{3}{10}$ (n) $\frac{7}{10}$ (o) $\frac{2}{5}$ (p) $\frac{2}{8}$

    (q) $\frac{4}{10}$ (r) $\frac{2}{8}$ (s) $\frac{5}{12}$ (t) $\frac{3}{12}$

4. (a)   (b)

    (c)   (d)

    (e)   (f)

    (g)   (h)

    (i)   (j)

    (k) 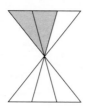   (l)

5. (a) Color $\frac{1}{3}$ (b) Color $\frac{1}{8}$

    (c) Color $\frac{2}{6}$ (d) Color $\frac{5}{12}$

    (e) Color $\frac{2}{9}$ (f) Color $\frac{3}{11}$

    (g) Color $\frac{6}{10}$ (h) Color $\frac{4}{9}$

    (i) Color $\frac{6}{12}$ (j) Color $\frac{5}{8}$

6. (a) Color $\frac{2}{3}$ (b) Color $\frac{7}{11}$

    (c) Color $\frac{6}{9}$ (d) Color $\frac{3}{5}$

    (e) Color $\frac{8}{12}$ (f) Color $\frac{4}{5}$

    (g) Color $\frac{9}{12}$ (h) Color $\frac{1}{7}$

    (i) Color $\frac{3}{5}$ (j) Color $\frac{3}{11}$

7. (a) $\frac{3}{12}$ (b) $\frac{5}{10}$

    (c) $\frac{7}{9}$ (d) $\frac{5}{8}$

    (e) $\frac{3}{7}$ (f) $\frac{5}{6}$

    (g) $\frac{1}{5}$ (h) $\frac{1}{3}$

8. (a) 1, 8   (b) $\frac{2}{11}$

    (c) $\frac{5}{12}$ (d) $\frac{5}{8}$

    (e) $\frac{3}{7}$ (f) $\frac{3}{4}$

    (g) $\frac{9}{10}$ (h) $\frac{3}{11}$

    (i) 10   (j) 5

    (k) $\frac{5}{8}$ (l) 7

    (m) 7   (n) $\frac{5}{7}$

    (o) $\frac{3}{8}$ (p) $\frac{5}{10}$

    (q) $\frac{2}{12}$ (r) $\frac{4}{11}$

9. (a) $\frac{1}{11}$, $\frac{1}{10}$, $\frac{1}{9}$, $\frac{1}{6}$

    (b) $\frac{7}{11}$, $\frac{7}{9}$, $\frac{7}{8}$, $\frac{7}{7}$

    (c) $\frac{4}{12}$, $\frac{4}{11}$, $\frac{4}{8}$, $\frac{4}{6}$

    (d) $\frac{5}{12}$, $\frac{5}{11}$, $\frac{5}{9}$, $\frac{5}{8}$

    (e) $\frac{1}{12}$, $\frac{1}{11}$, $\frac{1}{7}$, $\frac{1}{6}$

10. (a) $\frac{2}{3}$, $\frac{2}{5}$, $\frac{2}{7}$, $\frac{2}{11}$

(b) $\dfrac{3}{4}, \dfrac{3}{6}, \dfrac{3}{7}, \dfrac{3}{8}$

(c) $\dfrac{9}{9}, \dfrac{9}{10}, \dfrac{9}{11}, \dfrac{9}{12}$

(d) $\dfrac{1}{3}, \dfrac{1}{4}, \dfrac{1}{5}, \dfrac{1}{7}$

(e) $\dfrac{5}{8}, \dfrac{5}{9}, \dfrac{5}{11}, \dfrac{5}{12}$

Word Problems

1. $\dfrac{5}{12}$

2. (a) 4   (b) $\dfrac{1}{4}$

3. (a) 4 days   (b) $\dfrac{3}{12}$

4. (a) 5   (b) $\dfrac{4}{5}$

Take the Challenge!

(a) 72	(b) 64	(c) 90
(d) 32	(e) 96	(f) 40
(g) 64	(h) 96	(i) 96
(j) 162	(k) 128	(l) 216

Topic 5: Time

1.

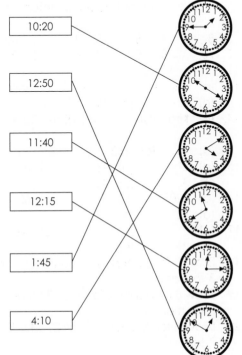

| 10:20 |
| 12:50 |
| 11:40 |
| 12:15 |
| 1:45 |
| 4:10 |

2. (a) 6:50   (b) 4:05
   (c) 9:00   (d) 5:55
   (e) 12:20   (f) 11:40
   (g) 8:30   (h) 1:15

3. (a) Eight   (b) two
   (c) Five   (d) ten
   (e) Twenty-five   (f) Twenty-five
   (g) Fifteen   (h) seven

4. (a)   (b)

(c) (d)

(e) (f)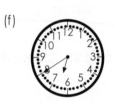

5. (a) (b)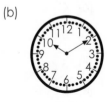

(c) (d)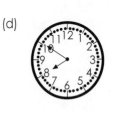

(e) 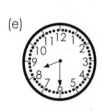 (f)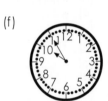

137

6. (a) 6:50 am   (b) 1:30 pm
   (c) 5:45 pm   (d) 1:55 pm
   (e) 9:35 am   (f) 10:45 am
   (g) 5:20 pm   (h) 11:58 pm
   (i) 11:40 am   (j) 12:20 am
7. (a) 11:00 am   (b) 12:00 noon
   (c) 2:00 pm   (d) 5:00 pm
   (e) 12:30 pm   (f) 3:30 am
   (g) 7:30 pm   (h) 10:00 pm
   (i) 2:00 pm   (j) 6:30 am

Word Problems
1. 7:45 am
2. (a) 11:30 am   (b) 12:00 noon
3. (a) 1:45 pm   (b) 3:45 pm

Take the Challenge!
1. 3 pm   2. 3 pm
3. 7 pm   4. 12:30 pm
5. 12:15 pm   6. 4:45 pm
7. 12:10 pm   8. 6:05 am
9. 8:35 pm   10. 3:15 pm

Topic 6:   Capacity
1. (a) B, C   (b) B
   (c) A, B   (d) C or B
   (e) C
2. (a) 3 ℓ (b) $2\frac{1}{2}$ ℓ

   (c) 3 ℓ (d) 7 ℓ

   (e) 2 ℓ
3. (a) 8 ℓ (b) 14 ℓ
   (c) 12 gal   (d) 23 qt
   (e) 25 ℓ (f) 45 ℓ
4. (a) 9   (b) 5
   (c) 2   (d) 28
5. (a) tray   (b) 8
   (c) 6
6. (a) frying pan (b) pot
   (c) 6
7. (a) X, Y   (b) 16
   (c) 12   (d) 18
8. (a) 3   (b) 1
   (c) 1   (d) 9
9. (a) 3   (b) 6
   (c) 3   (d) 1
10. (a) 2   (b) 4
    (c) 4   (d) 14

11. (a) 10   (b) 90
    (c) 60   (d) 2
12. (a) 1   (b) 20
    (c) 7   (d) 40
13. (a) 2   (b) 4
    (c) 4   (d) 40

Word Problems
1. 9 ℓ 2. 3 ℓ
3. 2 ℓ 4. 6 pt
5. 45 gal
6. (a) 9 c   (b) $6
7. (a) 244 ℓ (b) 55 ℓ
8. (a) 11 gal   (b) 14 gal

Take the Challenge!
1. (a) B, C   (b) 4 gallons
2. Amount of water in Tank D = 28 ℓ
   Amount of water in Tank A = 28 ℓ ÷ 4
                             = 7 ℓ
   Amount of water in Tank B = 7 ℓ – 4 ℓ
                             = 3 ℓ
   Amount of water in Tank C = 28 ℓ – 3 ℓ
                             = 25 ℓ

Topic 7:   Graphs
1. Color 8 daffodils; 7 roses; 7 daisies;
   5 butterflies; 6 bees; 5 snails
2. Color 2 tour buses; 1 double-deck bus;
   4 cars; 2 cement trucks; 5 motorbikes;
   1 van
3. 8   4. 18   5. 20   6. 40
7. 70   8. 10   9. 2   10. 9
11. 7   12. 8
13. (a) Joyce   (b) Jolin   (c) Jolin
    (d) 6   (e) 19
14. (a) Kiro (b) 5   (c) Kate, Karen

    (d) 15   (e) 165
15. (a) E   (b) 16   (c) A
    (d) 3   (e) 40
16. (a) 120   (b) 5   (c) 60
    (d) 60   (e) 170
17. (a) 2   (b) 9   (c) Wendy
    (d) 21   (e) 99
18. Draw 3 for Joshua; 8 for John; 9 for Jax;
    3 for Jason
19. Draw 8 for apple; 2 for pear; 7 for orange;
    2 for mango
20. Draw 6 for A; 3 for B; 2 for C; 5 for D;
    7 for E

21. Draw 4 for Carla; 3 for Laura; 2 for Kaylie; 5 for Juan; 7 for Paul
22. Draw 8 for Linda; 9 for Fiona; 10 for Kim; 6 for Ron; 5 for Norman; 7 for Colin

Topic 8: Geometry

1. (a) curved line   (b) straight line
   (c) curved line   (d) curved line
   (e) curved line   (f) straight line
   (g) straight line   (h) curved line
   (i) straight line   (j) curved line
2. (a) 8; 0   (b) 2; 2   (c) 2; 2
   (d) 5; 2   (e) 8; 4
3. (a)

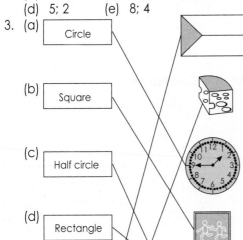

4. (a) circle   (b) square
   (c) rectangle   (d) half circle
   (e) triangle
   (f) quarter circle
5. (a) 6, 8, 2, 11, 3
   (b) 7, 6, 8, 0, 14, 4
   (c) 8, 2, 2, 3, 4, 8
6. (a)

   (b)

   (c)

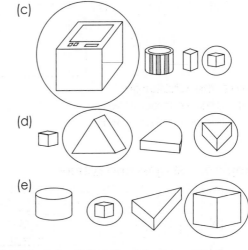

   (d)

   (e)

7. (a) 2; 1 (b) 6; 0 (c) 6 (d) 5
   (e) 2 (f) 5 (g) rectangles
   (h) 7 (i) 5 (j) A
8. (a)

   (b)

   (c)

   (d)

   (e)

9. (a)   (b)

   (c)   (d)

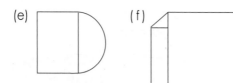

(e) (f)

Take the Challenge!
1. Infinite number of ways
2. Infinite number of ways
3. 15

Topic 9:   Shapes and Patterns

1.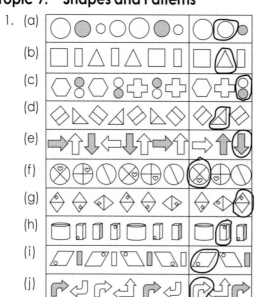

2. (a) (b) (c) (d) (e) (f) (g) (h) (i) (j)

3. (a) (b) (c) (d) (e) (f)

(g) 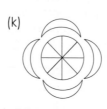 (h)

(i) (j)

(k) (l)

Take the Challenge!

1. (a)

   (b)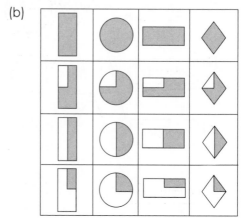

2. 10
3.

End-Of-Year Review
Part 1

1. 462	2. 29
3. 295	4. 4
5. (a) 177	(b) 835
6. 6	7. 109
8. 3	9. 7
10. 16	11. 10, 5
12. 9	13. 4
14. 12	

15. (a) B   (b) C
16. (a) ft   (b) lb
    (c) in.   (d) oz
17. ●────────────────────
18. (a) 4   (b) 5
    (c) 6   (d) 15
19. 28
20. (a) eraser, ruler
    (b) sharpeners
    (c) 175   (d) 1.15
21. 425   22. 4.38
23. 14   24. $613.02
25. $1.50   26. 1.37
27. $\frac{1}{10}, \frac{1}{8}, \frac{1}{7}, \frac{1}{3}, \frac{1}{2}$ 28. $\frac{7}{12}$
29. $\frac{6}{11}$ 30. 24

31.

32. 20   33. 2:25
34. (a) 5   (b) 3
35. quarter circle, triangle, half circle
36. (a) 3   (b) 1
37. (a) 8   (b) Mei
    (c) 5   (d) 72

38.
      39. A = 28, B = 9

40. 3

Part 2
41. $7   42. 727
43. 351 g   44. 24
45. 95¢   46. $\frac{2}{8}$
47. 7 yd
48. (a) 4   (b) $32
49. 368   50. 75¢

More Challenging Problems
1. (a) The first 10 flowers (2 red, 3 yellow and 5 green flowers) can be considered as 1 group. There are 10 groups altogether.
10 × 3 = 30 yellow flowers.

(b) No. of flowers in the first 8 groups
= 8 × 10 = 80.
The colour of the next 7 flowers are 2 red, 3 yellow, followed by 2 green ones.
The 87th flower is a green one.
2. 100 ÷ 10 – 1 = 9
3.
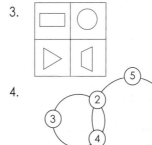
4.

5. 100 – 80 = 20; 20 ÷ 2 = 10; 10 + 5 = 15
100 – 80 – 15 = 5 pages
6. 6 + 7 = 13; 4 × 5 = 20
7. 702
8. (a)
```
  1 0 0 0    Sum of the 7 digits
–       1    = 1 + 0 + 0 + 0 + 9 + 9 + 9
─────────
  9 9 9      = 28
```

(b) Some possible ways are:
```
    6 4          9 5
+   8 5      +   5 4
───────      ───────
  1 4 9        1 4 9
```

Sum of the 5 digits = 23

9. 20 – 19 = 1, 18 – 17 = 1, 16 – 15 = 1, and so on.
Hence there are 10 ones altogether.
The sum is 10.
10. 10 + 13 – 11 = 12; 13 – 12 + 10 = 11
11. There are 7 different amount of money.

12. From the first diagram,

○○○ = ●●
      = 12 + 12
      = 24
    ○ = 8 g

From the second diagram,

▭ ▭ = ● ○ ○
      = 12 + 8 + 8
      = 28
   ▭ = 14 g

○ = 8 g,   ▭ = 14 g

13. (a) △ + △ = 24 – 18 = 6
           △ = 3
    ▭ + ▭ + 3 + 3 = 18
         ▭ + ▭ = 12
             ▭ = 6

  (b) ○ represents 5 times the number for ▽,

As 20 can be 1 × 20, 2 × 10, 4 × 5, 5 × 4, 10 × 2 or 20 × 1, only 10 × 2 = 20 will satisfy ○ × ▽ = 20.

○ = 10, ▽ = 2.

14. 10 ÷ (6 – 1) = 2 m; 2 × (18 – 1) = 34 m

15. (a)

  (b)

  (c)

or

16. (a) The beads are grouped in fours:

○○○●

The 22nd bead is white in color.
The 28th bead is black in color.

  (b) The beads are gouped in fives:

○○●●●

The 34th bead is black in color.
The 51st bead is white in color.

17.

18.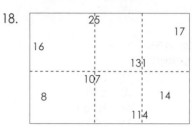

19. (a) 495   (b) 671

20. Z = $\frac{1}{6}$

21. 14 + 16 = 30
12 + 18 = 30
30 × 6 = 180

22. 3 × 4 = A
    A = 12
B × 4 = 28
    B = 7

23.

Height	Name of Boy
64 in.	David
60 in.	Clive
57 in.	Anthony
51 in.	Bobby

24.

Number of kittens	Number of ears	Number of legs	How many more legs than ears?
2	4	8	8 – 4 = 4
3	6	12	12 – 6 = 6

There are 3 kittens.